For Raydean,

partner and colleague in

the
strange
calling,

with good memories,
high hopes,
and boundless love.

Grace and peace,
John and Helen

Dedicated to those who,
by their example and encouragement,
first taught me how to listen to the strange calling

Loyd Bates
D. J. Bowden
Kenwood Bryant
Paul Burns
Otis Collier
Harry Emerson Fosdick
R. Benjamin Garrison
Richard E. Hamilton
H. Grady Hardin
Douglas Jackson
F. T. Johnson
E. Stanley Jones
Halford Luccock
Gene Matthews
Merrill McFall
Richard Campbell Raines
David Shipley
Wilbur Teasley

the strange calling

John Robert McFarland

SMYTH&HELWYS
PUBLISHING, INCORPORATED   MACON, GEORGIA
WWW.HELWYS.COM

Credits: "Fly Balls in the Graveyard," Christian Ministry (May-June 1996); "Leaving Chrisney," Christian Ministry (March-April 1993); "For Pete's Sake," Pulpit Digest (October 1965); "Publish or Parish: Commentary," Christian Ministry (March-April 1990); "Protestants Behind Bars," Christian Ministry (November-December 1997); "The Tall-Girl Bride," Christian Ministry (May-June 1998); "Desperately Seeking Thorndyke," Illinois Times (14-20 December 1989); "A View from the Bed" Christian Ministry (May-June 1991); "Love & Baseball," Fan: A Baseball Magazine (Summer 1997); "In the Balcony, Not Being a Bishop," Sharing the Practice: The Journal of the Academy of Parish Clergy (December 1995); "But Did You Have a Good Time?" Christian Ministry (July-August 1993); Now That I Have Cancer I Am Whole: Meditations for Cancer Patients and Those Who Love Them (Kansas City: Andrews and McMeel, 1993/New York: HarperAudio, 1993/Mason City IA: Night Song Press, 1997).

Smyth & Helwys Publishing, Inc.
6316 Peake Road
Macon, Georgia 31210-3960
1-800-757-3016
ISBN 1-57312-273-4
© 1999 by Smyth & Helwys Publishing
All rights reserved.
Printed in the United States of America.

John Robert McFarland

The paper used in this publication meets the minimum
requirements of American National Standard for Information
Sciences—Permanence of Paper for Printed Library Materials.
ANSI Z39.48–1984. (alk. paper)

Library of Congress Cataloging-in-Publication Data

McFarland, John Robert.
    The strange calling / John Robert McFarland.
    p.   cm.
    1. McFarland, John Robert.
    2. Methodist Church—United States—Clergy Biography.
    3. Clergy—Appointment, call, and election.
    I. Title.
    BX8495.M385A3   1999
    287'.6'092—dc21
    [B]   99-20557
                                               CIP
ISBN 1-57312-273-4

Contents

@cknowledgments

Pastoring is a special relationship. Folk let you into their lives through doorways that are usually locked and barred. I've been honored by thousands of persons, young and old, who have shared their joys and sorrows with me. I thank them all.

I also thank several persons who were kind enough to read this book when it was in manuscript form. They are:

- Dave Barry, Pulitzer prize-winning humorist and author, and the grandson, son, and brother of Presbyterian pastors
- Kim Egolf-Fox, American Baptist pastor and church school curriculum author
- Bob Hammel, the dean of Indiana sportswriters, author, and Presbyterian layman
- Garrett Keizer, Vermont high school teacher, Episcopal lay pastor, and author
- F. Dean Lueking, pastor of Grace Lutheran Church in River Forest, Illinois, for 40 years, author, and now professor at the Lutheran Seminary in Slovakia
- Elaine Palencia, author, lecturer, poet, and compassionate doubter/believer
- John J. Shaffer, United Methodist missionary and pastor
- William Powell Tuck, Baptist pastor, preaching professor, and author

The book is much better because of their suggestions. Any problems or mistakes that haunt the pages, however, are strictly the responsibility of . . . Dave Barry.

the ⓢtrange calling

Ministers are supposed to be "called" to that vocation by God. No one quite understands what "called" means, or how "the call" is accomplished, but nobody wants a minister who decided to be one just for the big bucks and easy workload. So when a candidate for ministry comes forth, s/he is invariably asked, "Do you have 'the call'?" Of course, the ministry isn't the only profession to which people feel called, so adjectives are applied to distinguish between calls and callings.

When I was still new to the ministry, I read a novel entitled *The High Calling*, by James Street. I knew before I pulled it off the library shelf that it was about a minister. That's how the ministry was known then, as "the high calling." I wanted to believe I had received a high calling. I knew it was a peculiar calling, but "high"? The way my call came . . . well, it seemed more like a "strange" calling.

The images of ministry in our society swing in a very short arc from the lovable but inept Father Mulcahy of M*A*S*H to the unlovable and equally inept Jimmy Swaggart. Because I knew nothing about ministers when I agreed to be one and had never seen any at work, except on Sunday mornings, I have made a point throughout my career to observe clergy with a critical but open eye. Neither Mulcahy nor Swaggart resemble any of the clergypersons I have watched so carefully over the years.

Thus, I hope these stories will show what really happens when a person thinks he or she hears the strange calling, and answers it. They are not just for pastors and church people. I hope that "cultured despisers" of the ministry will also read the stories and learn some truth about the people who live in the pulpit.

Story is first-level language, the text, the "what happened." Commentary is second-level language, reflection on what happened. As I have written, I have tried to use first-level language, to tell the story as it happened with a minimum of reflection and commentary. I understand, though, that in some cases a reader might want to know more about the context of a story—how I happened to be a part of it or what conclusions I drew from it. So, I have included some chapters that are not really stories. I think of them as commentaries or what happened in between times.

You can probably understand the stories without understanding all the church terms, too. But in case you want to check something out, there is a glossary at the end of the book. In addition, I have used the terms for ethnic groups that were common at the time of each story. For instance, African-Americans will appear as Negroes or blacks in certain stories. I've also used the names current at the time for gender groups. For instance, when I went to college, female students were "girls" or "coeds." ("Women" were mothers or secretaries or professors.) Male students were "boys" or "guys." ("Men" were fathers or janitors or professors.)

There are only a few people, I think, who would be embarrassed by the word-videos I have taken of them for these pages. There are several others who, although they look just fine, need to have their identities fuzzed over to protect their privacy, as in those television shots where everyone is clearly defined except for one face. To all these persons I have given new names. The first time I mention one of them, I mark his or her fictional name with an *asterisk. The non-asterisk folk are called by their own names.

fly ball⑤
in the graveyard

Kenny was the only left-handed batter in the church. That meant he was the only one who could foul the ball off just right so it would hit the women's outhouse when one of the girls was in there. A good line drive off the warped boards of the little white one-holer would not only rattle the vent pipe in its tin roof, but it would provoke a shriek of protest from Wanda or Darlene or whoever else had the misfortune, or the instinct, to get in there just before Kenny batted. The rest of us boys envied Kenny.

It was the annual Memorial Day softball game, between the men and the boys of the Forsythe Methodist Church. The softball game was a tradition, which meant it had also happened the year before. In a church anything that's happened for two years in a row is a tradition.

We had moved to the Forsythe community in February, just after I was ten years old. I did not know about traditions. I assumed I was taking up position in a game that had gone on forever.

After Sunday School and worship, the women who lived close enough raised high dust on the gravel roads as they quickly drove home to pull deviled eggs from refrigerators and hot casseroles from ovens. And they raised more high dust as they raced back to the church basement. Other women were already waving Betty Crocker wands and producing chocolate cakes and cherry pies and pickled beets and plates of fried chicken from out of car trunks. People brought their own plates and forks and iced tea glasses. Folks like the Heathmans and the Blairs always brought extras for the loose boys, the boys like me, who came to church without their families.

Forsythe was an open-country church, just a little white frame one-room building on a hill with a cemetery on either side and two little white outhouses behind. Tall, old oak trees surrounded the church building and guarded it against the humid breath of summer. A division of cedars flanked the graveyard, standing strong against the frozen breath of winter. The nearest house was half a mile down the gravel road. Still, we always said "The Forsythe Community" when we told people where we lived. Those fiercely independent dirt farmers and factory workers belonged to one another and shared an identity as surely as any ethnic ghetto in a city.

I knew a little about cities. We had moved from Oxford, Ohio, to Indianapolis when I was four. I attended Lucretia Mott Public School No. 3 from first grade through fifth. I was thoroughly a city boy when we moved to the Forsythe community, adept at dashing down alleys to escape neighborhood bullies, used to dodging gum wads on concrete sidewalks as I maneuvered Washington Street to go see the Saturday afternoon serial at the Tacoma Theater, able to dodge drunks staggering out of taverns, accustomed to walking to the library or to church. The only horses I had seen were in the movies. Now I was surrounded by them. My family didn't even own a car. I saddled up "Old Prince," our plow horse, to ride to the homes of friends for barnyard basketball games. The only day of the week I rode in a car was Sunday, when I walked up the road to the Heathmans and rode to church with them as one of the church's loose boys.

The first item of business for us boys on any "Lord's Day" was Sunday School, a time, we thought, for discussing "The Phantom" comic strip. Most of us in the country got our Sunday newspaper through the mail on Monday. John, however, had a bachelor uncle who lived in town. On Sundays he bought a newspaper right out of a box on Main Street, then came to John's house for breakfast. Thus, John knew that day's "Phantom" installment and could relay it to us, leading to endless Phantom futuring. Well, actually it wasn't endless, just until Mary Louise Hopkins, our teacher, arrived and made us discuss The (Holy) Ghost instead of The Phantom.

Sunday School started with "opening exercises." People called out the numbers of their favorite hymns until we had sung three or four. The "favorites list" consisted of only about ten hymns, anyway, so by the end of any month, we were repeating. Then came announcements and the birthday bank. On a birthday the celebrant, young or old, had to walk up to the little bank shaped like a church building and deposit the number of cents equaling the number of years, preferably in pennies, so everyone could count. Older (over 40) women just wadded up a dollar bill and stuffed it down the little crack in the church roof, figuring the extra cents were a small price to pay for privacy.

After opening exercises we boys were always the first ones in class, rushing down the basement steps to our pew in the corner, immediately engaged in earnest discussion of the perils of our hero and his disturbingly shapely girlfriend.

Mostly, the loose boys were brought to church by neighbors, but sometimes we walked or rode our bikes or horses to be there. Yes, it was the quickest way to get the news of The Phantom, but there was something else, something hard to explain that brought us to church. Boys of any age are often seen as more trouble than joy. They are not always wanted. The Forsythe people seemed to want us, especially those of us who had no reason to be wanted anywhere else. (In every church I've pastored I've tried to see to it that my congregation *wanted* the loose girls and boys; it wasn't always an easy task.)

The Forsythe folk were good enough to want us, even when we sang. At worship we sat together, with no parent nearby to rap a knee or sling a disapproving glance. We sang the hymns with more gusto than anyone could possibly want. No song leader ever had to urge us to sing louder. We tried to outdo one another in volume until the other worshipers couldn't even hear the twin pianos, until they stared at us in amazement, wanting, I'm sure, to tell us to "can it," and unwilling to for fear that we would take it as a hurt and not come back. I doubt they understood what made us sing so loudly, so crazily, belting out "Sweet Hour of Prayer" more like it was "Wild Hour of Dare." Those good people, however, were willing to endure hearing loss before they'd take a chance on driving away their loose boys.

When my theological alma mater created a scholarship in my name, 47 years after I became a loose boy at Forsythe church, it was those good folks in that tiny open-country church who made the largest contribution to the endowment.

Most worship services start with a "praise" movement of some sort, usually a hymn. The true praise time on the Sunday of the Memorial Day picnic, however, was the time of moving down the serving line on either side of the long food-laden tables. Praise for the cooking, praise for the eating. Men remembered loudly how much some other man had eaten at the last potluck. Women remarked loudly on how delicious the rolls or the potato salad, brought by a rival cook, must surely be.

We boys just picked out our favorites, chicken legs and pie slabs, and piled high our plates. We knew we'd need all our energy for the softball game when the eating was done.

We played the ballgame behind the church building, mostly between the outhouses and the cemetery. That space wasn't quite large enough, however. Thus, the men's outhouse was first base. Second base couldn't be angled over and back between first and third like a regular diamond, because of the shape of the cemetery, so it was just farther down the hill on beyond first.

It was a long run from second to third, but third base was easy to see. Third base was the preacher. He had two responsibilities there. One was to keep balls that got through the infielders from going into the cemetery. The other was to grab the men as they got to him in the course of their ponderous base running. The men were heavy hitters and, although they were slow runners, especially after rounding the potluck table and second base, it took us boys a long time to retrieve the ball and get it back to the infield. The preacher would hold the men as long as he could to give us boys a better chance.

When I heard my strange call to ministry, that was the job description as I had seen it at Forsythe Church: preach, eat a lot, respect the graveyard, and even up the sides.

Left field was in the graveyard itself. We were supposed to try not to hit the ball there, since the preacher couldn't cover the whole left side of the field and keep every ball out of it. We also knew we really shouldn't be dashing around the gravestones, over the bodies of the ancestors of those who now played ball beside their graves when the men were at bat and we were in the field. I don't recall, however, that anyone got particularly upset when the ball did get in among the graves.

Thus I learned about sin from playing ball beside the cemetery. You are supposed to avoid it, but if you do get into it, don't get worked up about it. Just throw the ball to the preacher and get out of there as quickly as possible.

I was 10 years old. I was the new kid, just one of the loose boys. I knew very little of sin or how to play left field in a cemetery. But because I was the new kid, that's where I was put—out in left field.

Later, when I was in high school and college, I played first base. It's the natural position for a tall, slow, heavy hitter. When I became a minister, however, the call included a move to third base, where I still play. It's the natural position for a preacher, a "reaction position" where you "guard the line." It's called "the hot corner."

At 10, though, I was out in left field. Left field was dangerous, out there amongst all those gravestones. Because I was new, I didn't know the accepted method of playing in that venue, which was to stand and watch the ball land, then carefully work one's way between the stones and pick it up and throw it in. Playing ball was serious business to me, joyful business, business I'd rather do even than eat fried chicken, but still serious. So when a ball was hit to me, I threw caution to the wind in the oaks and cedars around me and ran like a holy terrier through the graveyard, vaulting the lower stones, one eye on the terrain and one on the ball, occasionally even catching one on the fly.

The spectators were amazed—whether at my prowess or at my desecration of the graves and of tradition, I still am not certain. They weren't quite sure whether I was brave or stupid. Neither was I.

It has marked my career, that fuzzy line between bravery and stupidity. I've always felt that I was playing in the margin, a loose boy, at the edge of the graveyard, not quite sure where the game of the living ended and that of the dead began, just happy to be where I was wanted, glad to be in the game.

loo⑤e boys

I don't know why we had so many loose boys at Forsythe. I'm sure each of us had a different story to account for why we were there by ourselves. Mine was simple: my parents did not take me and my sisters and my brother to church because they did not go to church. They did not go anywhere. They did not want to face people. They were ashamed of Father's blindness, of our poverty, of being on welfare.

My father had lost his eyesight in an industrial accident in Indianapolis. The accident was not his fault, but his company fired him because he could no longer do his job. He received no pension, no benefits, no nothing except that his fellow-workers "passed the hat."

No one would hire a blind man. The now oft-threatened federal "security net" was not in place then. Some states had fairly supportive policies in dealing with people who had suffered physical or social catastrophes, but Indiana wasn't one of them.

Unable to find work in Indianapolis, my parents decided to return to Gibson County, where we could count on the kindness of family and the comfort of familiarity. My father had grown up on a farm near Oakland City in the days of horse-drawn plows and hand-milked cows. Later he read a book entitled *Five Acres and Independence*. He thought that with his memory and hard work and my 10-year-old eyes to guide him, we could make a living on the five acres we could afford to buy with its gap-sided barn and cockeyed chicken house and scraggle of apple trees and muddy little pond.

Father wanted to return to the lifestyle of his boyhood, one he thought he could work successfully without his eyesight. The Gibson County he had left in 1928, however, was not the one we found when we returned. We were probably the only family in the county without a car, the only farmers without a tractor.[1] We had electricity in the house, but not in the barn. There we used a kerosene lamp. We had a horse for plowing and pulling our old converted "Double Cola" wagon when we took feed to the mill in town. Mother did not go anywhere because she refused to endure the humiliation (and exposure to the elements and bad springs) of riding on the wagon.

We had neither indoor plumbing nor fixtures. We had a well (for drinking water) and a cistern (for wash water), but we had to carry in the water in galvanized buckets and carry it out again in older buckets when it had been used. We cooked and heated with wood and coal. Towns had water systems and gas for central heating. Other country people, like ourselves, might have wells, but they had plumbing to bring the water into their houses, and most of them had indoor bathrooms. Many were converting coal stoves to gas for central heating. My family still did not have those simple, expectable amenities when I went off to Indiana University in 1955.

Five acres did not lead to independence. Before long, my mother applied for welfare. The day the social worker came, Father went out into the barn and cried. We survived on Aid to Dependent Children in an area where "welfarechisler" goes together as one word, just like "yankee" goes together with another word in the South. There were two places, though, where financial status didn't count—the school and the church. My classmates and teachers were enthusiastically aware that if you got the most answers right, you had the best score, regardless of the number of patches on your pants.[2] At Forsythe, the people went out of their way to be sure the loose and the lost were welcomed and included. It's not surprising that I have spent my life in school and church, usually together.

notes

[1]Some of the older farmers still plowed with horses in 1947, but even they switched to tractors within a few years.

[2]I told this story at a class reunion a few years ago. Later, Paula Eskew Nossett said to my wife, "We respected him so much, we had no idea he was poor." This says much more about Paula and the rest of my classmates and my teachers than it does about me.

the miracle

The baseball season wasn't over yet when the telephone rang, shrilled with the hollow echo of my sister's name— two longs and two shorts, marking us off from the other 13 families on our "party" line.

"Mary V. is sick," the telephone said. "She's in the hospital. It just came on so fast. No one knows what's wrong. Her kidneys are failing. There are holes in the sack around her heart. Her lungs are filling up with fluid. The doctors say she has only three hours to three days to live. You'd better get down here fast."

She was 19 years old.

Mary V. was only four and one-half years older than I, but she was really a second mother to me. Sometimes she was my primary mother.

From the time she was a little girl, Mary V. had an ability to take life as it came and deal with it. One Sunday, when she was four, Mother asked Uncle Randall to take her to Sunday School. Knowing Mother was Methodist, Uncle Randall took Mary V. to the Methodist church. When it came time to pick her up, Uncle Bob was sent. He assumed she had gone to the Presbyterian Sunday School, his mother's church. After frantically searching up and down the student-lined streets of Oxford, Ohio, Uncle Bob finally found her sitting on the steps of the Methodist church, calmly "reading" her Sunday School paper, knowing someone would come for her.

As a first grader, if she didn't like the menu at school, she walked downtown and bought her lunch at a diner, sometimes explaining that she had no money but that the owner could go down to McFarland's Service Station and get it from her father. As a second-grader, when she got tired of McGuffy's school one day but didn't know how to get home, she just walked out and took a taxi to Cedar Crest, the big house on the edge of town where grandparents and uncles and parents and children all lived together. She walked into the house and announced that someone should go out and pay the taxi driver.

In a childhood that was often a jungle of chaos and fear for me, she was a clearing of stability and joy.

It was a mournful day for me, then, when she graduated from high school and went off to the big city to take up a career as a telephone operator. The big city was Evansville, Indiana. It was only 30 miles away from Oakland City. For a poor family without a car, though, it might as well have been another country.

The day of the telephone call, Uncle Harvey drove from Evansville in his bright red car. He got to our farm faster than anyone thought possible. Mother and Daddy were ready. Mother had thrown clothes into a suitcase for Margey and Jimmy, eight and nine years younger than I. Mary V. had been a mother to them, too. They had all piled into Uncle Harvey's car and headed back toward the highway before the dust from his arrival had settled.

I watched them go through the dust and through the haze of my own eyes. I alone was left . . . because someone had to stay behind to "do the chores."

We lived on a "one" farm—one horse, one cow, one pig, one duck, one chicken, one apple tree, one. . . . When you live on a "one" farm, somebody always has to be there to do the chores, especially to milk the cow. For the three hours to three days it would take my sister to die, I was that somebody.

I was alone, as I often was on the farm, but now I was lonely, too. Alone and lonely, but relieved. Relieved that I would not watch my sister die. Alone and lonely and relieved and afraid. Afraid of death. Alone and lonely and relieved and afraid and ashamed, ashamed of my fear, ashamed of the yellow streak that ran all the way from Deaconess Hospital, down Indiana Highway 57, 30 miles to the middle of my back. My sister would die without a word or a hug from me, just because I was afraid. Better, though, to be alone and lonely and afraid and ashamed than to see your world die.

I was 14 years old.

I went to the barn to do the chores. As I sat on an upturned bucket to milk the cow, I prayed.

I had learned at church how to pray. I could see the church building through a gap in the barn wall even as I prayed, little Forsythe Church, half a mile away across the fields, standing bold against the brassy evening sun. I learned grace at Forsythe church, but I had also learned there the accounting theory of faith, that if you prayed just right, if you offered God just what He[1] wanted, you could do a deal with God.

To do a deal, however, you have to have something to offer in exchange for what you want. God's not going to just hand out one-way contracts. The only thing I had to offer was me, my own life. What could God possibly want with a 14-year-old farm boy? Well, to be a minister. That was the thing God "called" people for, wasn't it, to be preachers? I did a deal.

I said it, right out loud. "God, if you'll save Mary V.'s life, I'll become a minister."

My voice must have been rather low; the cow didn't even turn around.

The three hours passed. The three days passed. Mary V. got well. She didn't take up her bed, but she walked. Her mysterious illness fled from her body as quickly as it had come upon her.

The doctors said, "We don't know what happened. We didn't have anything to do with it. We just gave her painkillers, waiting for her to die." Then they used that fateful word. These men of science actually spoke it out loud. "It was a miracle," they said.

I, alone, knew what had made the miracle. . . .

· · · · · ·

I'd been tricked! It never occurred to me that I would have to keep that bargain. The people in the white coats had said she would die! They were *doctors*. They knew everything. How could they be so wrong?

Well, for one thing, they were up against God. If they couldn't outgun God, what chance did I have?

But I didn't want to be a preacher! I was going to be a journalist and smoke Pall Malls and wear one of those hats with the press passes stuck in the band. I was going to go to Indiana University, to the Ernie Pyle School of Journalism. I was going to be the next Ernie Pyle! What did I know about being a preacher?

For the first time in my life, I had to think theologically: Had God made Mary V. sick to get me to go into the ministry? Would God have let her die if I hadn't done the deal? Would God come back and get her if I didn't keep the Faustian bargain foisted upon me?

I can't remember who was preaching at Forsythe right then, whether it was the postmaster from Oakland City or the factory worker from Evansville or the student from Asbury Seminary. Whoever it was, I couldn't ask him any of these questions. Everybody knows how stupid preachers are about theology.

So I went secretly to the only real theologian I knew, Aunt Nora. She played the organ at the Francisco Church, six miles away.

I told her the story of why Mary V. got well. Then I asked her the questions.

"Aunt Nora, did God make Mary V. sick to get me to go into the ministry?"

Aunt Nora smiled. "Yes," she said.

"Would God have let her die if I hadn't said I'd be a preacher?"

Aunt Nora's smile grew wider. "Yes," she said.

"Will God come back and get her if I don't do it?"

Aunt Nora was literally beaming now. "Oh, yes," she lilted.

There was one more question I didn't dare ask: Is a God like that worth serving? I was afraid I knew the answer, and I knew it wasn't the same as Aunt Nora's.

Through all the years Aunt Nora's smile never faded. She was always immensely proud of her nephew, the minister. She'd always wanted someone from the family to go into the ministry.

I didn't believe Aunt Nora, of course. How could any rational person believe in a God like that? I was only a 14-year-old farm boy, but I knew better than that. I have had to learn many times what Aunt Nora was trying to tell me, that however strange the form of the message, God is in charge.

It is what God told Job: "I'm God. You're not. Get used to it." When he heard it, Job pronounced himself satisfied. I wasn't satisfied yet. I hadn't suffered enough to understand.

I can't explain what happened the next summer, between my freshman and sophomore years at college. Maybe it was because Mary V. never got sick again. Even as I write this, she's the healthiest person I know. Maybe it was just because McFarlands are proud people, proud people who keep their bargains and their promises and their deals. Whatever it was, I knew, strange as the method had been, that I'd been called, and that there was no way to get dis-called. Listening to a Duke Ellington record on a humid summer night, I knew that God had called me. Alone and afraid and ashamed, I turned in my Speed-Grafix camera and my newspaperman's hat. I went into the ministry.[2]

notes

[1]There was definitely no question about God's gender in Gibson County, Indiana, in 1951!

[2]Tex Sample says, "Being called to the ministry is a little like throwing up. You can put it off for a while . . ."

the big ⑤tory

On the radio I listened to "The Big Story," sponsored, of course, by Pall Mall cigarettes. Each week's segment dramatized how a journalist had gotten his "big story." It sounded very romantic to me.

I wanted to be a journalist because I loved words and stories and radio, and because Uncle Bob and Uncle Randall and Uncle Mike were in the army. Indiana people were mighty proud of Ernie Pyle, a native son. I heard people say that Ernie Pyle's columns told the story of the army as it really was. That meant he was writing about my beloved uncles, telling their stories as they really were. What more noble task could there be than that?

I didn't keep the deal. I quit high school in February of my senior year and went to work in a factory. I wanted to get us off welfare, but it also gave me a chance to run around with my friends at night and drink turpentine-tasting machine coffee during the day in order to stay awake as I stared into my light to adjust electrical relays.

Some of my friends, like Jim Shaw, graduated, but didn't have a job or any plans. About the middle of July, bored with it all, Jim said, "Let's drive up to Indiana University on your day off and see if they'll let us in." It sounded like something to do.

They not only "let us in," but they also admitted me to the Residence Scholarship Program for "poor but highly motivated" students. In return for doing our own maid and janitorial work, we got free room and board. The boredom of the factory was a definite motivation toward something else. Equipped with nothing but hope, I figured I could get a job both to earn my tuition and keep my family off welfare.

The Residence Scholarship Program was in the east end of Linden Hall, an old wooden "bachelor officers quarters" building left over from World War II. The housing people agreed to put Jim in the west end of Linden where "regular" students lived. Two months later Jim and I started college. I was going to be a journalist. But I did watch my sister's health very closely.

leaving Chrisney

Dallas Browning was the District Superintendent (D.S.), the man in charge of all the Methodist churches for 30 miles around. Aunt Nora said I should go see him, let him know of my decision before I went back to college the next week. I made an appointment and drove our 1950 Chevy down to Evansville. The D.S. lived in a big house. He looked like he ate well. There was a new Buick in the driveway.[1] Maybe preaching wouldn't be so bad, I thought.

I told him I had decided to become a minister.

"You feel like God's called you?"

"Yes." I didn't tell him about Mary V.

"Where do you go to school?"

"I'll be a sophomore at I.U."

"Ever preached before?"

"No, but I took Speech 101 last year."

"Get a good grade?"

"A."

"Get good grades generally, do you?"

"All A's last semester." I didn't tell him about my disastrous first semester, which was over before I had realized school had begun.

"Good. I've got three churches, need a preacher who gets good grades. Only three months, 'til the preacher we're going to appoint there graduates from seminary in January, but it'll be good experience for you. You can come down on the weekends from Bloomington, spend the night in the parsonage, supply the pulpit on Sunday morning, be around for Sunday School, help with the youth group, find out what it's all about. Here's the name of the people for you to see when you get to town. I'll let them know you're coming." He wrote on a piece of blue paper that had his name at the top.

"You mean . . . right now?"

"Next Sunday. Oh, I know what you're thinking, but don't worry about that license to preach.[2] You're supposed to do the written work for it and all first, but you're getting good grades. You can do that later. I'll just go ahead and sign a license for you now."

I hadn't been thinking about the absence of a license to preach. I didn't even know such things existed. But he pulled a paper out of a drawer, asked me how to spell my name, signed his, handed it to me. I was a preacher.

What I had meant to say was that I hadn't really figured on starting my career so soon and that I had no way to get from Bloomington to Chrisney every weekend. I could hitchhike, as I did when I went home, but that wasn't a very reliable method. It also wasn't very seemly for a preacher. The D.S. didn't act worried about that, though, so I figured it was my problem.

"Dr. Browning seemed really impressed that I'm getting such good grades," I told my family that night over fried chicken and mashed potatoes.

"Hard to get anyone with any brains to be a preacher," my father observed.

Nonetheless, he helped me get my brother-in-law's 1948 Oldsmobile down off the concrete blocks in our barnyard. It had been there for two years, while Dick and Mary V. were with the Navy in Antigua. I wrote them and told Dick I needed to use it. He sold it to me for $50. My father got it running again. He was blind, and he hadn't gotten good grades, but he could make anything run.

I went to Chrisney the next Sunday, September 23, 1956. I didn't go to the church building first. Instead, I looked up the people whose names were on the piece of blue paper, Bob and Catherine Adams. She was little and cute and dark-haired. He was muscular and flat-topped and energetic. They were getting two grade-school-age boys and a little girl ready for church, but they sat me down, gave me a cup of coffee, told me about which church I was to go to first, and how to get there, in between tie tyings and curl combings.

I followed the directions, went to Crossroads, an open-country church, like Forsythe. The pianist wanted to know which hymns I wanted to sing. I hadn't thought about that. I looked at their hymnal. It was red. The hymnal at Forsythe was brown. I couldn't locate any hymns I knew. I told her maybe she should pick the hymns. A bumblebee came in through an open window while I was preaching and flew around my head. When it landed on the pulpit, I smashed it with the foreign hymnal. Everyone laughed; I figured my first sermon was a success.

I can't remember what I preached on September 23. I have the bulletin from that day, but no Scripture or sermon title is listed. My first notes are from October 14, my fourth Sunday on the Chrisney charge. That day I preached on Joshua 6:1-5, 20, using the title "God Will Show You the Way." The title sums up the sermon quite well. The sermon is nicely outlined, with Roman numerals and capital letters and Arabic numerals, just like Speech 101. I cited Joshua, Paul and his Macedonian call, Peter Marshall, Emerson, a painting, a road sign, and an actress named Marjorie Rambeau. I wasn't worried about running out of material; I possessed a stack of my grandmother's old *Reader's Digest*s.

After Crossroads I returned to Chrisney. I suggested the same hymns we had sung at the first service, but they had a blue hymnal. I preached the same sermon, though, and was surprised to find it wasn't the same. After Chrisney, I drove out to Bloomfield, another open country church, and preached the same different sermon for the third time that morning.

Then it was time for dinner at the Adams house. Throughout my time at Chrisney the Adams family was uncommonly kind to me, inviting me into their home and family for Friday and Saturday night suppers and Sunday dinners. I sometimes think I learned more about churches from them in three months than I did from seminary in three years. They explained the churches to me, which women would not work with which other women. Their sons thought my flat-top was cool and started referring to me as "the knothead." They gave me a key to the parsonage.

After my last class on Friday afternoon, I would load up my Oldsmobile and drive the 90 miles to Chrisney. I lived there from Friday evening to Sunday afternoon in the empty, six-room parsonage. It contained only two pieces of furniture—a metal folding chair and a narrow, metal camp bed. I would stand my Samsonite suitcase on end and balance my portable typewriter on it to have a desk. I ate my breakfast and lunch of peanut butter and white bread standing at the counter in the kitchen. To a 19-year-old, it was intensely romantic and infinitely sad.

It was in that house that I heard the uncertain steps of Bob Adams on the porch one dark Friday night, just a month after I started riding the Chrisney circuit. There was no porch light, just the glow from a bare bulb in the empty living room when I opened the door. I had never seen Bob like that before, lost in shadows, out-of-place in his own town. I could smell evil and agony in the dry October air.

"Three of the high school boys were going down to Tell City to the movie," he blurted out. "One of them was driving his dad's new '56 Ford. They hit a bridge abutment. The speedometer was stuck at 120."

My heart sank in misery and flared into anger. Boys just a few years younger than I. How could they do something like that? I was glad Bob had come to tell me; I'd have to incorporate it into Sunday's sermon, along with the quotes from Emerson and the *Reader's Digest.*

He just stood there, though, and a stirring in my stomach told me he had come for something more than adding to my sermon.

"One of them was Billy Quick. You haven't met the Quicks yet. They don't come to church much, but Billy's one of ours. His parents and the rest of the family have gathered down at their house. They're waiting for you to come comfort them."

"Come comfort them?" I didn't know anything about comfort. I didn't even know about real sadness. No one close to me had ever died. I'd been a 16-year-old pallbearer at my grandfather's funeral, the only one I'd ever been to, but he died full of years and several hundred miles away. I wasn't a pastor; I was just a weekend preacher. I felt like Peter O'Toole's character in the movie *My Favorite Year*, when he learned he had to go on live: "I'm not an actor! I'm a movie star!" I was called to preach, not to comfort people.

I thought seriously about getting into my old Oldsmobile right then. I carried a five-gallon can of oil in the trunk and had to stop every 50 miles to pour a quart in the motor. I figured there was enough left in that can to get me back to Bloomington one more time, and that's all I cared about.

Bob, however, got me down to the Quick's house by a simple stratagem. He just told me I had to go. Although I didn't put the word with it then, that was the moment I learned a minister is a professional. You "play with pain." That's the highest accolade a professional athlete can receive, what marks the amateurs from the pros. You "play with pain." You do what must be done because it must be done. You don't let your wounds get in the way of another's healing, your doubts get in the way of another's faith, your fears get in the way of another's hope.

Besides, I didn't know how to say "no" to this man who had been so kind to me. I was reasonably sure, though, that this was a sign from God that I had totally misread my call. The "GPC" on my horizon really did mean "Go Plow Corn," instead of "Go Preach Christ" (or, since I was a journalism major, "Go Publish Corn.")[3]

The Quick house was small and simple—cracked linoleum on the floors, coal stoves in each room, an outhouse in the back. A dozen "old" people—the ages of my parents and grandparents—sat solemnly and quietly around the walls of the main room. The men wore high-top work shoes and overalls. The women were draped in feed sack housedresses and black oxfords. No one wept. No one spoke. They just stared at me.

I was the parson, the person, *the* person, the one who had come to speak. I was "the man." But I knew "the man" was shouted in the voice of Nathan pointing out an impostor—"Thou art the man."

I spoke. I babbled on. I said everything I could think of on the subjects of death and eternal life. It must have taken 30 seconds. Worst of all, I remembered some terribly sentimental tripe I'd read, in the *Reader's Digest*, I think, about how God always chooses the best roses for the heavenly garden, so I blamed this tragedy on God and the horticultural arrogance of the divine will.

I wasn't asked to do the funeral. It would have interfered with my class schedule. The resident Protestant pastor from the Evangelical and Reformed church did the funerals of both the Protestant boys.

Then I left Chrisney. Left before my three months were up, at the end of November. The way Dallas Browning saw it, the Bloomington D.S. "stole" me. F. T. Johnson offered me another three-point charge 20 miles, only half-a-quart of oil, away from Bloomington. It was a month before the new pastor would arrive, but I left Chrisney going down that big hill at the north end of town heading toward Bloomington, seeing only the leafless canes of wild blackberry bushes (and an Olds-stream of oil smoke) in my rear-view mirror.

I knew it wasn't my fault. I'd done the best I could. I wasn't prepared or educated for dealing with death, for being a pastor to people in need. I should never have been put in such a position. The District Superintendent should never have sent me there. Bob Adams should never have stepped up on the parsonage porch that night. God should never have called me.

The family of Billy Quick deserved better, and I couldn't give it. Experience and education have made me a good pastor over the course of the 500 deaths of my subsequent career. Whenever anyone has told me how well I did a funeral, though, I have whispered to myself, "Yes, but you weren't there on that October night in '56, before I left Chrisney."

I had been wrong when I saw Dallas Browning's new car, thinking that maybe preaching wouldn't be so bad. He'd been in the ministry for a long time. He'd paid a high price for that Buick.

notes

[1] Early on, I was told that a DS needed three Bs to be successful. A big Buick. (Many meetings to drive to.) A big briefcase (Many documents to carry to many meetings.) A big bladder. (Many cups of coffee at the many meetings.)

[2] A "license to preach" was entirely Methodist, not a state license.

[3] An old preacher joke: A farmer was working in the fields when he saw the letters GPC written in clouds in the sky. He was sure they meant "Go Preach Christ," so he went into the ministry. After an undistinguished career, he told of how he had been called. "Apparently," someone observed, "GPC meant Go Plow Corn."

c⊙untry churches
and the inner city

I continued to preach where F. T. Johnson appointed me, at Solsberry, Koleen, and Mineral, little churches 16 to 35 miles from my dorm. They were far enough apart that I couldn't preach at all of them each Sunday. They held Sunday School every Sunday morning, but the following worship schedule: Solsberry on the first and third Sunday mornings of the month and the second and fourth Sunday evenings. Koleen on the second and fourth Sunday mornings and first Sunday evening. Mineral on the second and fourth Sunday mornings and the third Sunday evening. Twice in my three years on the Solsberry Circuit, I went to the wrong church.

Fifth Sundays were impossible to work in and remember, so I had those weekends off. Helen and I took advantage of that situation; we married on a fifth Sunday. The apocryphal story that I proposed by saying, "There's a fifth Sunday coming up, so why don't we get married?" is only partially true.

I had begun to read about the inner-city ministry of attorney and theologian William Stringfellow and of the East Harlem Protestant Parish. A weekend workcamp with the Indiana University Wesley Foundation at Howell Neighborhood House in Chicago convinced me that the inner city was the place I should be in ministry.

At the end of my junior year at I.U., I took the summer off from my churches and went to Chicago.

the ⓡumble

I didn't know Randy that well. We'd only been working together a few weeks. But when you're standing in the middle of the street, facing down rival gangs that are intent on having a rumble, anybody's back against your own is a comfort. Randy and I were quite literally back to back.

He was facing the Mexican kids, not because he habloed any Español. I was facing the Negro kids, not because I understood any jive. We had simply pulled on jeans and shoes and run down from the third floor of Howell House where we'd been sleeping. The gangs were advancing on each other from either end of the block. Howell House was right in the middle. Now, so were Randy and I.

The gangs had names, of course, but I can't recall them. I'm not sure we knew even then. In the house we just referred to them as the Negro kids and the Mexican kids and the dark Puerto Rican kids and the light Puerto Rican kids. There were enough white kids in the neighborhood for a gang, but they were Wops and Polacks and Bohunks,[1] identified too much by nationality to get along in a gang just because their skin was the same color. I'd left my glasses upstairs when I'd jumped out of bed, but in the blurry dark I recognized kids I knew, kids I coached in basketball, kids I tutored in summer school, kids I took on trips to the Lincoln Zoo and to Wrigley Field. I didn't know the gang names, but I knew the names of the kids.

"Benny, Ty, Bobby, you're waking up the neighborhood. This is only going to get you in trouble. The police are on their way. Clear out quick. Come back tomorrow, and we'll talk about it."

I was just stringing together anything I could think of, beginning to realize that the middle of Racine Street, in the middle of the night, in the middle of a gang fight, was not a good place to be. Over my shoulder I could hear Randy talking to the Mexicans, in his soft Arkansas drawl, the same sort of stuff, each of us pitching our voices like we were speaking only to our gang, hissing instead of shouting, trying to get them to focus on us instead of on the other gang, trying to make them think, make them talk, use their mouths instead of their knives and chains. This was 1958, long before the gun warfare of current gangs.

My gang hissed back at me, loud enough for the Mexicans to hear. "They in our 'hood, Man. This our turf. Tell them to get out."

"This is Bohunk land," I heard an English speaker among the Mexicans say to Randy. "We got as much right to be here as anybody." There were Spanish mutterings also, affirmations I took it, of what the English speaker had said.

He was right; it was Bohemian territory. At one time the Pilsen neighborhood of Chicago housed more Bohemians than any place other than Prague. I preached on Sunday mornings at Wycliffe Methodist Church as one of its first English-speaking pastors. But the neighborhood's Bohemian solidarity had long since begun to crack. Many of the second and third generations had already moved out to Berwyn. Pilson had become a polyglot neighborhood. Anyone could claim it. It was up for grabs, and the teen gangs were intent on grabbing it for themselves. I figured I'd put my grab in, too.

"This isn't anybody's turf," I heard myself say. "This is Howell House territory. Nobody rumbles on our block. We don't care what color you are or where you come from. That's a church. Anytime you're in sight of that building, you act like you're in church."

Most of the kids didn't know it was a church. It didn't look like a church building because it wasn't one. It was a three-story settlement house with a plain brick façade and a blacktop playground. The Presbyterian congregation was small. Its worshipers met in the big, flat-floored general purpose room with the cracked linoleum, sitting on folding metal chairs.

The eyes of the kids automatically went to the building. They slowed down to look at it, then . . .

"That not a church, man. That a house, Howell House."

"That's a house, alright, the house of the Lord. A Presbyterian church. Reverend Nead is the preacher. You know him. You see him come in there all the time. It's the Presbyterians who make the basketball possible, man. They're the ones who pay for that playground right there, where your little brothers and sisters come. This is a special church. They don't just pray in there. They do all the classes and all the fun stuff, too. They make it all happen here. You mess around here, man, there's not gonna be anything happenin'."

I made it sound like it was just the local Presbyterians who did the whole settlement house program. Actually Howell Presbyterian Church was separate from Howell House. Don Nead was only the local pastor. Jon Regier was the director of Howell House. Presbyterians from all over the Chicago area supported Howell House and its permanent staff of five social workers and its eight summer college student interns. Randy and I were two of the interns. I did not intend, however, to stand in the middle of the street and try to explain Presbyterian organizational structure to rival gangs. I wasn't sure one could do that even to Presbyterians. I just wanted to stop this rumble from happening, keep kids I knew from hurting one another.

Randy and I continued to stand there, waiting, not sure what was going to happen. Finally we heard a voice from a window on the third floor, the floor of the staff's sleeping rooms and living and dining rooms.

"Are you guys going to stand out there all night?"

The voice was soft, probably Marian or Shirley or Nancy.

Randy was even taller than my 6'1", and good looking to boot, but he couldn't see a bus on a sunny day. I was without my glasses. We peered into the darkness.

"They all left, you idiots. Too bad, too. They should have beaten some sense into your college heads. Don't they teach you anything practical at those institutions of so-called higher learning? Running out in the middle of the street . . ."

The voice trailed off as it went back to its own room, but there was no question about who it belonged to—Connie, professional social worker, the mother of us all. Connie was really old, maybe even 40. She didn't suffer fools gladly.

Carolyn and Barbara had come downstairs, too, and had watched from the office windows. They opened the door for us, and we all trudged back up to the third floor. I wanted to sit up a while, calm down a little, talk about what had happened, but a rumble was just a rumble. We all had to get up and be back on the streets the next morning, back on the playground, back in the classrooms on the second floor, back in the gym in the basement. Without a word, the girls all returned to their beds.

Randy and I went back to our room, too, on the rear of the third floor, and dropped onto our lumpy mattresses. After a while I heard the deep breathing that signaled he was asleep. I crept out of my bed and stared down into the alley. I was glad there had been no rumble, pleased no one had gotten hurt, happy I was still in one piece. But I was disappointed, too. I had wanted to hear Marian tell me how heroic I was. Instead, I had only heard Connie tell me how stupid I was.

note

¹Their terms, but we usually used them, too. We were aware that we shouldn't, but it was easier and descriptive.

"welcome, touri⑤ts. welcome to America!"

"It's wonderful work you're doing here—whatever it is."

That's what the Presbyterian lady from Oak Park told me after I had walked her group through the building and talked about our various activities. I knew how she felt. That was my impression, too. It was wonderful work—whatever it was.

I think I had gone to Howell House to do that wonderful work because Sid Denham had climbed up on his chair when he answered Roger's question. Our Wesley Foundation had spent a work-camp weekend at Howell House, painting and doing general maintenance, learning about inner-city ministry.

"How come you're doing all this instead of preaching the gospel?" Roger had asked.

Sid pushed back from the long, scarred table, jumped his Hush Puppies up onto the rickety wooden folding chair, teetered there like a thrush in the wind, reached out his arms to encompass everything in the room and everything beyond its walls, and shouted to us all: "This *is* the gospel!"

It seemed to me that a man who would stand on a chair like that to answer a question like that had to know some truth. Now that I was there, though, now that I was doing the work, now that I was coaching basketball and supervising the playground and walking the streets with my bag of toys, and taking kids to the zoo, and leading the Wahoo Indian Tribe, I wasn't as sure. It was wonderful work, but was it the gospel?

That question had never occurred to me before, not before running into "fundamentalists" in college and questioners like Roger. Were the fundamentalists, as I knew them, right? Were preaching and living the gospel just a matter of praying and preaching and studying the Bible and converting others to "a personal relationship with Jesus Christ?"

I had always assumed that being a Christian meant standing with and working for the marginal and dispossessed, the ones Jesus called "the widows and orphans." Why did I believe that? Forsythe Church? Maybe. That congregation believed in taking care of people. Exposure to the Bible? Possibly, through my Sunday School teachers and the preachers I'd heard, but I hadn't studied the Bible much on my own at that time. Concern for others like myself, because I had grown up marginally, on welfare, a loose boy? If that were true, was my gospel just an extension of selfishness?

I was more sure of the gospel content of what I did on Sunday mornings. First, I preached at the Wycliffe Methodist Church. Then I preached at the glorious old Halstead Street Institutional Church, a combination church and settlement house. It had been a great force for faith and service through generations, but the new interstate highways had wiped out almost the entire neighborhood it had served and left it with about 20 members to scatter around the Gothic sanctuary that would seat 500, not counting the balcony. Its swimming pool and gymnasium and offices and club and meeting and class and cooking and music rooms went unused all week. It was open only on Sunday mornings, and it wouldn't even have had a preacher if the Methodist kid from Indiana University hadn't been working in a summer intern program a few miles away in a Presbyterian settlement house in another neighborhood.

I was immensely proud, though, of preaching in that mighty old church building. I would hurry over from Wycliffe as quickly as possible to get there early so I could sit in the pastor's study with its fireplace and three walls of glass-fronted bookcases, and imagine what it must have been like to be the minister in the bustling heyday of that grand institutional church. Then I would preach to the scattered worshipers and empty pews. Afterwards I'd walk the lady with the keys on her slow and sad lockup rounds.

Sunday mornings ended with me fixing lunch for the other summer interns[1] and staff members, most of whom had slept in. It got me a lot of praise. I felt wondrously righteous, very proud of my humility in being both preacher to my neighborhoods and servant to my colleagues.

One Sunday Randy and Dan went to my churches with me. Instead of going home for lunch, we went down to Maxwell Street, that marvelous polyglot market. There was no auto traffic. Vendors spread their wares, including items such as watches that were Bulova on the outside and Timex on the inside, on blankets on the street and sidewalks. Portable stalls filled every inch of the rest of the space. Merchants called from the narrow doors of the permanent shops along the streets. A carnival of smells and sounds I had never smelled or heard before swirled around us in the heat of the summer morning. I could hear Ketelby's "In a Persian Market" playing in my head.

We turned a corner and ran into a Polish sausage stand. A wizened little man inside it, with blackened teeth and an accent just off the boat, took one look at us, in our crewcuts and narrow ties, and cried out, "Welcome, tourists. Welcome to America!"

He was right. This was his America, not mine. I was a tourist in this urban land. I didn't belong there, and never would, but I didn't know that then. It took me a long time to figure out where I did belong.

In the meantime I worked at learning the ways of Christian presence in the inner city.

In the mornings I met with my clubs, the seven to nine-year-old girls who didn't have a name for their group and the seven to nine-year-old boys who did. They were the Wahoo Indian Tribe, and you always knew when they were around by their shrill cries of "Waaahhooooo!" In both groups we cooked and read and told stories, especially about the Bible. The little girls and I had a spirited discussion one day about whether "that prayer" said "lead us *not* into temptation" or "lead us *into* temptation." If the majority rules, Jesus suggested we should pray to be led into temptation, I suppose to toughen us up through experience. Lily, the nine-year-old leader of the pack, went on to explain that Jesus had taught that because all the people had been dancing around and singing the blues and he had to do something to get them back into line.

I also worked with the girls drama group. They came up with a dramatic play they called "Voodoo Woman." It was simple in concept. One girl was the voodoo woman. The object was for her to grab each of the other girls, throw them to the floor, and strangle them. The ones who had not been strangled could "revive" the ones who had been subjected to the voodoo woman, thus returning them to the game. I noted in my written report, "The realism is frightening."

I walked the streets each afternoon with a bag of toys. Wherever children gathered, I took out tops and jump-ropes and paddle balls, and we played a while. Then I invited them to Howell House, to come to the clubs. I was an evangelist. It's difficult now to imagine how I got away with that. These days parents will call police if they see a strange young man approaching their children with toys in a bag. Back then I was the one who had to watch out for my safety, not the children.

In the evenings I played basketball with the older boys or chaperoned teen dances.

Sometimes the clubs took field trips. We often took them places, just to find out what the rest of the world was like. That was before the days of omnipresent television, and most of the children had never been out of their own neighborhoods. One day I took the Wahoos downtown. On the bus, people were generally indulgent as they shrilled their Wahoo identity call.

We went into the Marshall Field store. The little boys especially liked the women's lingerie department, calling out loudly for me to come see some piece of incomprehensible apparel. I got them out of there as quickly as possible and onto the down escalator. I was first, and then came Bob Jones. He tripped getting off and fell right at the bottom of the escalator. Before I could get him up, the next boy tripped over Bob and added to the pile. I started pulling at various limbs but hadn't moved the heap much when the third boy, and then the fourth, piled on, each with a wild cry of "Waahooo!" There were about a dozen boys. They all whooped their Wahoo cry and jumped on the pile. They were followed by two elderly ladies of the silk dress, North Shore variety. With nowhere else to go, they put their purses above their heads, yelled "Waahhoooo!" and piled on. I'll always be grateful to those women.

The eight-year-old Bob Jones always made things interesting. Once we took all the clubs together to Brookfield Zoo. We were in front of the tiger pits when one of the Wahoos tugged at my t-shirt.

"Look, Mr. John. Look where Bob is."

I have no idea how he got in there, but Bob was definitely in the tiger pit. Not very far in, and it was a big pit, natural style, instead of a cage. The tiger didn't seem much interested in a small dark boy, for which I was grateful. I started to climb over the barriers to go get Bob, hoping the tiger would be no more interested in a tall light morsel than it was in the small dark version.

"Don't," hissed Barbara. "You'll stir it up. Wait for the keeper."

Waiting seemed like a good idea, but Shirley was already trying to talk Bob out with remarkable absence of success. How long could we depend on the tiger to ignore someone like Bob? Besides, patience was not my strong suit. I went over the rocks and rails and dragged Bob out, hoping the tiger would realize I was too skinny to be much of a meal. The keeper came just in time to see me climbing out of the pit. He threw me out of the zoo, with the admonition that I was lucky he didn't have me arrested. I got off easy, even at that. When Bob bit the biceps of my fellow summer-staffer and sometime room-mate, Dan Larsen, Dan had to take sulfa for a month to counteract the infection.

One day we drove the kids up to Wisconsin for a week at summer camp. This was before the days of interstates. We wound our way along Lakeshore Drive and up through the mansions of Evanston, each one bigger and more impressive than its neighbor.

"Cripes, this must be where all the gangsters live," said one of the kids.

"What in the world do you mean?" I asked

"Why, who'd have enough money to live in a house like that except a gangster?

I tried to explain about education and hard work and capitalism. Later, I came to think the children were on to something. Didn't someone say, "Every great fortune starts with a crime"?

I know some folks who never made a fortune: Sid and Liz Denham, Carolyn Williams, Shirley Thompson, "Shep" (Ellsworth) and Tony Shepherd, Connie Perry, Jon Regier and his family. They were the permanent staff of Howell House. They put up with a lot, for little pay, to live where they were needed. They were uncommonly patient with those of us on summer staff. They are old people now. I hope they have good memories. I hope Sid is still able to get up on a chair in the nursing home and spread his wings and proclaim, "This *is* the gospel!" I hope he knows that he and the others made Howell House church for me as much as Forsythe or Wycliffe or Halstead Street.

note

[1]Barbara Bailey, Carel Diekerhof, Sigrid Koch, Dan Larsen, Randy Robertson, Marian Ure, Nancy Weesner

liberal(s)
don't get the girls

She pushed me away gently, her fingertips a velvet blow upon my quivering cheek. I could still taste her full and sweetened mouth upon my pale and uncertain lips, could still feel the pressure of her generous breast against my skinny chest. (Well, sure that's corny, but when you're 20—at least if you were 20 back in 1957—that's the way you think it, so that's the way you write it!)

Yes, in my brain I could still taste *Marie's lips and feel her bosom, but I was pretty sure those memories in my brain were all I was going to have in about 10 seconds. Our relationship had been stretched like a rubber band, ready to snap. I knew I was the one it would sting back on.

Not romantically strained, our romance was intense. Marie was certainly the most passionate girlfriend I'd ever had, certainly the only one who'd grabbed me and kissed me and held me so close I thought I'd explode, and kept on doing it night after night. That was all we did—kiss and hold. There was no question in either of our minds that "petting" and "making love" were to be reserved for marriage. But Marie was a warm-blooded girl. It was she who initiated our physical relationship and kept it going. I suppose I might have put a little more into it if I'd had to, but her need was enough for both of us.

I wasn't unaware that girls could be interested enough in the physical part of romance that they were willing to "do things." I didn't trust the tales of my dormmates, of course, about what girls would do. Even they didn't believe most of what they claimed they did. Alfred Kinsey had published his famous research into human sexuality at Indiana University only a few years before we matriculated there. One of his findings, according to someone in our dorm, was that the average college unmarried male, in our era, had sex 30 times a year. Upon hearing that, my roommate, Tom Cone, blurted out, "Somebody's doing it 60!" I took the number up to 90. We went around the dorm, doing our own research, and found that someone was doing it 1,920 times!

Still, I'd had some experience of "loose women." In my freshman year I had idolized *Julie, a sweet little blond, a church organist back in her hometown. We had dated a few times when one night we were sitting in a shadowed corner of the lounge in her dorm. She grabbed my hand and put it on her breast. I was sure she'd made a mistake. It was exciting. It was enticing. It was certainly inviting. I was sure, however, that the quickest way to lose a nice girl was to fool around. A nice girl wouldn't do a thing like that. I was absolutely sure Julie was a nice girl. If I mistook her intention, I'd get a slapped face and lonely Saturday nights. A couple of dates later, Julie dumped me, saying, "I'm afraid *you're* too nice for *me*." I was shocked and shattered, having lost the love of my life because I wouldn't feel her up. My roommate couldn't believe the depth of my idiocy.[1]

Despite my reluctance to get inside the clothing of my girlfriends, on the apparently mistaken assumption that they wanted to keep all garments in place, Marie and I did want physical intimacy, wanted it bad. I think Marie wanted it even more than I did, and I wanted it the proverbial 110%. We didn't talk about it, of course. We just sat in my scratched green Chevy and kissed and hugged and, in the apostle Paul's words, "burned."

Originally, I had thought Marie and I were just dating, but she seemed to have something else in mind. As one step after another led me closer to the slippery slope, I just got dragged along, not reluctantly, but like an ox that is being led to the pit and doesn't know enough to realize that the smell of barbecue sauce isn't really a good sign.

It wasn't that I was opposed to marriage. I wanted love, wanted closeness, wanted intimacy, wanted sex, wanted a family, as only a romantic idiot can want them. I knew marriage was the way to get the important things of life. I was also aware that it wouldn't do my career in ministry any harm, since an unmarried minister in those days was suspect in a dozen ways and considered a poor catch by a church. That way it got only one full-time church worker instead of the two-for-the-price-of-one that it was used to when a wife was thrown into the bargain, especially if she could sing or play the organ (one of the reasons I was drawn to Julie, I suppose).

Marie would make a good minister's wife. She didn't have a solo voice, but she could be a good choir member. She didn't play the organ, but she was of an obviously religious nature, so she'd be able to lead programs for the WSCS. I had no idea if she could cook for potlucks, and potlucks are very important in Methodism. (When our daughter, Kathleen, was asked by her Roman Catholic husband-to-be what one had to do to be a Methodist, she replied, "Believe in God, and have a 9x13 pan.") I assumed, however, that there was some kind of female cooking hormone that kicked in automatically when a woman married, so I wasn't much worried about the potlucks. Also, Marie was quite pretty, so the men of the church wouldn't have to worry about me fooling around with their wives.

Yes, a pretty girl, a passionate girl, a religious girl, an intelligent girl, a good prospect for a minister's wife all around. I wasn't sure, however, that she was a good wife prospect for *me*. I mean, wasn't love supposed to mean something more than a slaking of one's hormones and an asset to one's job? I didn't want to be an idiot again, though, and lose a girl because I wasn't "fast enough" for her. So we talked marriage, that magic doorway that would lead into the castle of physical love. Well, we didn't *talk* marriage, and we certainly didn't talk sex. We just assumed that since we wanted to have sex, we'd have to get married.

Without ever saying a thing to each other about actually getting married, we went to the home of friends, another student minister, and looked at their wedding photos. Marie and Pat spoke of colors and flowers while Vern and I sat there and grinned sort of stupidly at each other. We talked about housing for married students. We talked about having morning devotions together. . . .

That was when the problem came. I was all in favor of morning devotions. Marie and I, however, were on very different pages of the book. Morning devotions raised the issue of theology.

We had met at a gathering of the InterVarsity Christian Fellowship, IV for short. That was the way it was supposed to happen. I had gone there to meet "nice" girls. Everyone on campus knew the IV girls were "nice." They were also a bit frustrating, because along with being nice, they were, mostly, quite attractive. A whole passel of good-looking girls who won't fool around is a great frustration to college boys. It sounded like the perfect place to me. I was bound to find a girl there who wouldn't throw me out the car door because I wouldn't throw her over the car seat.

I had gone to IV in the first place because I had fallen for an "older woman." *Patricia was probably 23, already a nurse, back at school working on an advanced degree. I wanted to hear a particular minister in town preach, so I had gone to an evening service at his church. I was disappointed; he wasn't preaching that night. Instead, three students from IV were there to "share their religious experiences." *Patricia was one of them. I was no longer disappointed. In fact, I'm not sure I thought of that minister or his preaching ever again. Instead, I started going to IV meetings.

Patricia agreed to go out with me a few times, but she was a serious woman, and I was a romantic child. She marched on resolutely toward her goal of becoming a missionary nurse. Without malice, I just got bumped aside. But Marie was standing there, waiting to grab me when the bump came.

Now, the road was getting bumpy again. I liked the IV girls, but the IV theology and I didn't get along very well.

The reason I thought Marie might not be the wife for *me* had more to do with theology than with romance.

Remember that I had been thinking theologically since I was 14, since I'd had to confront the God who performed miracles people both wanted and didn't want. I didn't know many theological terms. Those would come later, when I took undergraduate courses in the "History of Christian Thought" from D. J. Bowden, my first theological mentor. In my IV days, theologically, I was like a person who is pushed into a soccer match without knowing the rules or the strategy. You can run up and down the field and kick the ball once in a while, but you're not sure what the other players are doing or why. You certainly don't understand why the referee occasionally throws up an arm and everyone runs over to the corner or turns around and goes the other way.

One night at the IV Bible study, *Lawrence, the leader for the week, proclaimed that God does not hear the prayers of sinners, and that we knew this was so because it was in the New Testament. The other students all nodded approval. I said that sounded rather strange, and not very biblical, since God wouldn't hear any prayers at all then, because we are all sinners. The protagonist of God's deafness explained that some of us were not sinners, that some of us—obviously not including me—were "saved." I replied that even salvation didn't seem to make us perfect, and surely God would have mercy upon sinners, since there wasn't anyone else who needed mercy, and how could anyone be saved if God wouldn't listen to the prayers of a sinner asking to be saved.

I was silenced, however, by the bottom line: it's in the Bible, so it has to be true. I was reminded of that night many years later when I saw a bumper sticker proclaiming: "God said it. I believe it. That settles it." That night, however, I was also silenced by the fact that no one else in the whole group, including Marie, seemed to find my "rational" approach very appealing. In fact, "rational" was said with something very close to a sneer, which struck me as a rather unkind attitude for the "saved" to take.

When I got back to my dorm room, I decided to look up this passage about God not hearing the prayers of sinners for myself. All I could remember from the discussion was that it was somewhere in the New Testament. I started with Matthew and read. Through Mark. Through Luke. On to the ninth chapter of John, the story of the man born blind, whom Jesus healed. In his defense of Jesus to the Pharisees the now-sighted man said, "We know that God does not listen to sinners" (v. 31), proving, as far as he was concerned, that Jesus was not a sinner, since God obviously answered him. It was not Jesus claiming that God doesn't hear sinners. John was pointing out that such an idea was a false theology used by those arrayed against Jesus.

It was late, but I called up Lawrence and asked him if John 9:31 were the Bible passage he'd had in mind. He was quite pleased at my diligence and told me that yes, I had indeed come to the correct passage.

"But that's not what that passage is saying," I said.

"What do you mean?"

"Well, those Pharisees are claiming Jesus is a sinner, and . . ."

I don't remember the rest of the conversation. Lawrence would not be moved. It was *in the Bible,* and even though the force of the story was the opposite of how he was using it, that made no difference. To him, all the sentences of the Bible could be cut apart from one another, thrown into a pail, and pulled out in any order, and each would have the same authority as any other.

That made no sense to me, which, according to my IV friends, was my first mistake, trying to make sense, trying to be "rational." My second mistake was my narrative inclination. I lived by story. I knew you couldn't cut up the books of my childhood, books such as Don Lang's *Tramp, The Sheep Dog* or Cornelia Meigs' *Mother Makes Christmas,* or the books of college such as Faulkner's *Dry September* or Stendahl's *The Red and the Black,* and pull the sentences out in any order and still have a story. If you had no story, you had no life. It would be 20 years later before I knew enough to understand that I had been, all along, a "narrative theologian."

All Methodists, and the followers of John Wesley whatever they may call themselves, come to know what the great Wesleyan scholar Albert Outler[2] termed "The Wesleyan Quadrilateral" for understanding and living the Christian faith: scripture, reason, tradition, and experience. Each one is important and necessary. No single element, including Scripture, can stand alone, claiming that it does not need the others, for even Scripture is always communicated to us through reason and tradition and experience. Jesus said that we are to love God with all our *mind* and heart and soul and strength.[4] When I was 20, I still did not know that Wesley, through Outler, had organized these elements so neatly in his quadrilateral, but I intuitively knew that they were all there, and all were necessary.

The IV folks, on the other hand, claimed to be "Scripture alone" believers. It was quite obvious to *me* that they interpreted the Bible through their own experiences and traditions and reason, even though their interpretations often seemed *un*reasonable to me. They denied, however, that they used anything but the Bible itself, that as the "saved," they got their understanding of the Bible directly from God, and if I disagreed with them, I obviously was neither saved nor in touch with God.

I pointed out that they often disagreed with one another, which meant at least some of them were getting wrong revelations. That "rational" approach, however, marked me increasingly as an outsider.

I also pointed out that the Bible was a story, just like life, that where something came in the story made a difference, that you couldn't pull out an introductory passage and put it in the conclusion and have it mean the same, or have it mean something in itself without the context from which it had come. That narrative approach also marked me as one beyond the pale. The Bible wasn't a story; it was a book of rules, each one of which held some objective "truth" that had nothing to do with where it came in the story.

I figured they might be right about me. There was a distinct possibility that I was neither saved nor on God's direct communication pipeline. After all, I was called to be a minister, not to be saved. I wasn't into all this religious thinking because I really wanted to be; I just didn't have a choice, because I was keeping a deal. I was beginning, though, privately, to doubt that I could be a minister at all if I had to believe this stuff or deal with people who did.

My doubts began to boil over into public because of the incident with *Susan.

I'm sure Susan was a real seeker. I didn't know her well, but I think she started coming to IV because, like almost all college students, she had religious questions. Also, like almost all college students, she was seeking community. She found community, but it was more than she could handle. Her new friends began to hammer at her. Her questions were irrelevant. IV had the truth, and all she had to do was believe it.

The meetings began to revolve around Susan. Susan was the subject of every prayer and every discussion. She would sit on the floor and cry, afraid to break away because she needed the friendships, but unable to claim the assurance she was constantly told would be hers if she just believed.

We were all told, out of her hearing, that we should go out of our way on campus to search for Susan, learn her routes to and from class and her dorm, so that each time we saw her we could call out to her that we were praying for her. I learned Susan's routes, not so I could tell Susan I was praying for her, but so I could worry about her. The worry wasn't hard; each day she looked more distraught. I tried to be upbeat, commenting on the beauty of the last leaves of autumn, on the busyness that surrounded midterm tests, hoping that such trivia would communicate my concern and get her mind onto something else than the absence of her salvation. She said she could neither eat nor sleep. Knowing nothing better to do, I suggested she get some rest and eat something. I also suggested that it would be okay, in order to get some rest, if she stopped coming to IV meetings. She didn't seem to hear.

Each night, before and after our sessions of kissing and planning marriage without talking about it, Marie insisted that we pray for Susan. I pointed out to her that I didn't think it was doing much good, that Susan looked pretty bad to me.

Marie took my fears to the leaders of the group. They assured her that Susan's discontent was a good sign, that she was "under conviction," that it was a necessary prelude for someone like Susan to go through the storm in order to reach the safe haven of salvation.

Instead, Susan reached the safe haven of the psych ward at the hospital. She never came back to college, or to IV.

The next meeting was dedicated to cursing the devil, since it was that evil one who had driven poor Susan to the psych ward. I more or less agreed, until I realized they meant that the devil had put Susan there in order to keep her away from IV, so that she could not be saved. At that point, I suggested it might be God who had put Susan in the psych ward to save her, and that if it were indeed the devil's work, the devil had had some help and it wasn't necessary to look far to see where it came from.

The next day they began to go out of their way on campus to cross my path and call out to me that they were praying for me.

I went to see Loyd Bates, the minister at the Wesley Foundation. I had been to WF only a couple of times, and I didn't mention it to anyone in IV, because there was some tension between the two groups. I'd met Loyd, though, and he seemed like a good person to ask for advice.

"Boy, are you in trouble," he said.

"What do you mean?"

"Everyone knows that if you're on IV's list, you've had it."

"Well, it's embarrassing to have them yelling that out at me all the time, when I'm walking with the guys from the dorm, but surely it's not so bad to be on a prayer list."

"You don't get it. Their prayer list is their ____ list."

The treatment I began to receive from IV seemed to confirm his statement.

I picked up Marie at her dorm one night. It was clear that something was going to be different. I'd never seen her cry before. She grabbed me and held me and hugged me. Then she pushed me away gently, her fingertips a velvet blow . . . well, you already read that part.

"I can't see you anymore," she said.

I was no little chagrined. Here was this beautiful, passionate girl . . . *another* beautiful, passionate girl I wasn't going to get to go to bed with. I was just a little bit relieved, though. I wouldn't have to go to IV anymore.

"But why?"

"You're too liberal for me."

That night, sitting on the fire escape of my dorm, shivering a little under an orange-gold harvest moon, I tried to figure out what a liberal was. I'd been too nice for one girl and too liberal for the next, which meant being nice and being liberal might be the same thing.

If I were a liberal, then this was the definition of the breed: A liberal wants to feel up his girlfriends but doesn't. A liberal keeps his bargains. A liberal doesn't think he has all the answers. A liberal is wary of those who do think they have all the answers. A liberal looks at the wider picture to get a better view of the smaller scene within, especially with the Bible. A liberal doesn't like to see people hounded into the psych ward. A liberal doesn't know what to do if he does see people being hounded into the psych ward. A liberal is stupidly romantic. A liberal never gets the girl.

It was about this time I discovered that little poem of Edwin Markham's:

> He drew a circle to shut me out,
> Heretic, rebel, a thing to flout,
> But love and I had the wit to win,
> We drew a circle that took him in.

That, I decided, must be the real mark of the liberal, the desire to bring people in rather than shut them out. Marie and her friends had hung the label of the outsider on me, that label of liberal, sort of like a secret sign on one's back that says "Kick Me." Maybe Marie had done me a favor, perhaps even more than if she'd gone to bed with me. Maybe I could draw circles that would take in even the folks of IV.

notes

[1] My roommate, C. Thomas Cone, a criminal lawyer, with whom I have nothing in common, except we love each other's wife and children, IU basketball, learning, and each other. We're still crazy after all these years, and he still can't believe the depths of my idiocies!

[2] One of my professors when I was a student at Perkins School of Theology at Southern Methodist University.

[3] I love the banner that proclaims, "Christ died to take away your sins, not your mind."

cookbook⒮
by flashlight

Helen and I married at the end of my senior year. Students were required to be out of their dorms within 24 hours of their last exam. Helen was stretching the time-line a bit. We were going to spend our first week of marriage in a borrowed apartment, across the street from her dormitory, but we couldn't get into it until after the wedding. We were planning to move her things across the street then.

When the dorm director discovered that Helen was over the 24-hour limit, she demanded that she move out immediately, two hours before the wedding. Helen rounded up her friends, who dashed up and down the hall, always on the lookout for the dorm director, and secreted her things in their own rooms.

In the process our wedding license was lost, until we found it later in one of the clandestinely retrieved boxes from the rooms of her friends. We "lived in sin" for two weeks, because *everyone* who had to sign the license had left Bloomington! Helen's roommate and maid of honor, Norma Sullivan, had gone to New York City to start a master's degree at Columbia University. My best man and uncle, John Hubert Pond, had returned to his home and lumber business in Francisco, Indiana. Even the minister, Richard Hamilton, had moved to a different church, one in Indianapolis, the day after our wedding. We sent the license to Uncle Johnny, who sent it to Norma, who sent it to Dick Hamilton, who sent it to us, and finally, officially, we were married.

When I left my dorm room and went out to my new, yellow English Ford to go to our wedding, the car wouldn't start; the transmission was locked up. I later learned that if you got onto the rear bumper and jumped up and down, you could dislodge the stuck transmission. I had to do that once with two little old church ladies in the back seat. They thought it was great fun. Not knowing that particular mechanical maneuver at wedding time, however, I dashed back into the dorm and grabbed the car keys of my old roommate, Tom Cone, leaving him to find a way to the church on his own.

Our friend, Bill C. Brown, was our photographer. When he took his film to be developed, he discovered that his camera shutter was broken; none of his pictures came out. The only photos we have of our wedding are two snapshots my Aunt Dorothy Pond took outside the church. We were never able to look back, so we've just always looked ahead.

I preached full-time on a three-church circuit while Helen finished her university degree. Or, perhaps it was her mother's degree. Georgia Mary Heltzel Karr was probably the best mother-in-law a man could have. Even if she had never done anything else for me, she sent her daughter to college.

Georgia had wanted to go to college herself. Her father, though, said such an idea was stupid; it was simply a waste of money to educate a girl. When Georgia's first daughter was born, she decided that the little girl with no middle name would go to college. To that end, she never allowed Helen into the kitchen or the sewing room; she was never to spend her time on domestic chores. Her one task was to study, to prepare herself for college. Helen, a good daughter, did as her mother directed. As a teenager, however, she secretly bought cookbooks, disguised them with the dust jackets of novels, and read them under the covers at night in the dim glow of a flashlight. She was valedictorian of her high school class in Gary, Indiana, of course, and didn't much care where she went to college, since it wasn't really her idea. Her mother said, "IU, not Purdue. Nice girls go to IU." In her heart she said, "Not Purdue, because it's a home ec school."

Naturally, when the counselor at IU asked Helen what her major would be, she said home economics. She studied cooking, sewing, child development—all the things she had been sent to college to avoid. She earned a bachelor's and a master's and has enough hours beyond for a doctorate. For 20 years she's taught home ec. She didn't learn anything about the subjects she teaches from Georgia or Earl Karr. From them she only learned about love. Of course, that's really what she teaches.

Danny's funeral

The February sky was gray that day, the day we buried *Danny. Gray like old ashes. Gray like old dreams.

We weren't supposed to be burying Danny. There wasn't anything wrong with him, not really. 16 years old. President of the junior class. First five on the basketball team. Kids like that get killed in car accidents. They don't die just because they catch a cold.

That's all it was, a cold. But it hung on, like ash-gray days in February hang on, until they add up and together become the longest month. February days and February nights hang on until they become a solid shield of gray around your heart.

Something in Danny had been making a gray shield, an armor plate that refused to let any medicine in to chase the germs away. The "cold" never became anything else, at least nothing else the doctors could put a name to. It just hung on, and so did Danny. Finally they took him to the big hospital where the professors worked. If anybody could find a cure, they could.

They couldn't. The cold hung on longer than Danny could. Danny died.

Danny's father had already lost his wife behind the gray shield. He'd lost his first son to the gray ghost of war. Now his last son, his baby, was gone. Gone behind the gray face of February.

I was Danny's pastor, his father's pastor, his church's pastor. I was the representative of God who went to see him in the big hospital. I told him jokes, talked about basketball, not believing he could really die, not wanting to see the fear of death in his young, brown eyes. Brown eyes going gray.

I didn't *want* to believe that Danny could die. Finally, though, there were no more jokes, nothing else to say about basketball. I did what pastors have to do, even if they're only

22, even if they're barely older than the kid in the bed, even if they've never been to theological school or seen another pastor at work.

I prayed with him, prayed that he would soon be well, that he would soon be home.

Danny died. The big hospital with all its professors and machines and medicines weren't able to keep him alive. I, with all my prayers and fears, I wasn't able to keep him alive, either.

Now I had to do his funeral.

Danny had never been to a funeral. His first funeral was his own. He was 16. I turned 23 while Danny was in the hospital. I'd been to two funerals.

My first funeral was that of my grandfather, Arthur Harrison McFarland, the second of three Arthur McFarlands. The first Arthur was killed at Gettysburg. The third Arthur, my cousin, was killed much later in another war; he died of AIDS. The second Arthur, my grandfather, went by Harry. During the depression, when I was very little, when my father couldn't find a job, we lived with Grandpa and Grandma Mc at Cedar Crest, the big old farm house at the edge of Oxford, Ohio.

Grandpa was the stationery engineer for the power plant at Western College. He'd learned to be an engineer by correspondence. Grandpa let me help him shell peas. He let me follow him around the yard when he pushed the old reel mower under the maple trees and around the iris beds. When my mother spanked me, for some imagined infraction, Grandpa went into the backyard and cried.

I was one of Grandpa's pallbearers, 16 years old. I was too nervous to remember anything of what the pastor had done or said at his funeral.

My second funeral, I was 20. I was a sophomore at Indiana University, but it wasn't Knight school then. Bobby wasn't even out of high school yet. Branch McCracken was the basketball coach. He'd already won two national championships. Burke Scott of Tell City and Dick Farley of Winslow were two of the stars of the 1953 championship team. My Oakland City team had played against them in high school. I knew basketball. I didn't know funerals.

I didn't know anything about funerals, but that didn't keep the old man from dying. He wasn't a member of the church. He was a sociable hermit. He had no family, so the neighbors arranged the funeral. He lived near the second of my three churches. I was the preacher there, so the people from that congregation called me up and told me to get into the green 1951 Chevy, for which I'd traded my green 1948 Oldsmobile, and come out and do his funeral. I couldn't figure out a way to say that I was a pastor who had no idea how to do a funeral.

I went to "Charlie Pat," Charles Patterson, a retired minister in my college town. I asked him how to do a funeral. He gave me *The Book of Worship* of our denomination and said, "Just do the service like it's printed." There were opening Scripture sentences and opening prayers and Old Testament readings and New Testament readings and closing prayers. He didn't mention that you were supposed to choose one of each. I read them all. It took an hour.

Still, it was a good funeral. The old man was full of years. We buried him out on the hillside beyond his cabin, beside his wife, under an apple tree that was in bloom.

A man and a woman sang together, sort of, ancient words on the soft spring air of an orchard hillside. You couldn't really call it a duet, but they sang the same words, mostly at the same time. There was no organ out under the white blooming apple tree, no piano, not even a guitar. They started flat and went downhill. Their voices were appropriate to the lyrics, mournful and thin. The birds chimed in, though, robins and cardinals and blackbirds and mockingbirds. It was quietly hopeful, peacefully joyful. There were no shades of gray.

I was 23. I'd been married less than a year. My part-time appointment had become full-time for a year so that my wife could finish her degree in home economics before I went to theological school to learn how to be the minister I was already expected to be.

There was no funeral home in the village, just a school and a store and a feed mill and two churches. The visitation was in Danny's living room, just 10 feet from his bedroom, where his high-top basketball shoes slouched still in the corner. The coffin was open. My new wife was from "da region" (as the citizens of the Lake Calumet region call it) from Gary, the city of steel mills. She'd never seen a coffin in a living room. She thought that with a coffin in it, the living room should be called something else, but she didn't know what.

When the afternoon of the funeral came, the funeral directors drove up from the county seat. The pallbearers went to Danny's living room. So did Danny's father and stepmother and sister. So did various other family members. So did I.

The funeral directors had grown up in our village. They were distant cousins of Danny's father. They acted like they didn't know what to do, being in Danny's home instead of in their funeral home. They finally closed the lid on the casket.

The pallbearers lined up, three on either side of the casket. Without a signal, they picked it up. The funeral directors told me to walk ahead of the casket. I stepped out the door of Danny's living room and down the street toward the church. The funeral directors and Danny's father and the rest of the folks from Danny's living room followed us.

We walked right down the middle of the unpaved street, the packed gray mud of February pulling in the sounds of our Sunday shoes, the hard gray sky of February pushing down upon our bare heads. I walked as upright as I could, my shoulders squared in my Uncle David's long black overcoat, glancing over my shoulder to be sure I didn't get too far ahead of the pallbearers, a character in a Bergman film, in black and white and gray.

As we passed the houses, the people inside were waiting for us. They came out of their living rooms and fell in at the back of the procession, shuffling along behind Danny's casket.

We passed the store and turned left, past the feed mill and over the railroad tracks. We turned right and came to the church. The others waited for us there, the ones who didn't live along the route of the casket. Finally came Danny's classmates, each one carrying a pot of the funeral flowers.

I went up the steps and down the center aisle of the church. The pallbearers followed. They placed Danny's casket on the rolling stand just in front of the center pulpit. The funeral directors took the pots of flowers from the high school juniors and placed them around the casket. They opened the lid to the casket again. I took off my uncle's coat and joined *Old Brother Matheny behind the pulpit.

That's what he was always called, Old Brother Matheny, this former pastor of the church. It was poor form for Danny's father to ask Old Brother Matheny to come back for Danny's funeral. It's never appropriate for a family to invite a former pastor of the church to return for a funeral or a wedding. The current pastor needs to preside over those rituals. Otherwise, she or he never becomes the pastor, not really. I knew that, but I was grateful they had asked Old Brother Matheny to come back. He really was old, older than my own father. Old Brother Matheny had done many funerals. His presence was a comfort not just to Danny's father and to the others who knew and remembered and loved him, but to me.

I read the Scriptures and the prayers from *The Book of Worship.* I didn't read them all this time.

Old Brother Matheny preached. He did not avoid the difficult questions, but waded into them with confidence and an open Bible and an old black suit. *Why did Danny die so young?* He did not know. *Did Danny or someone else sin so grievously against God that the transcendent One was exacting punishment?* No. *Is there more life for Danny?* Surely, although we have no idea what that is like. *Is God with us in this difficult time?* Yes. *Can we trust God, even though we don't understand?* Yes. *Does God really care about Danny and about us?* It's sometimes hard to believe, but yes, God cares.

I've preached at 500 funerals since Danny's. At every one, some way or another, I've had to answer those same questions. I'm now older than Old Brother Matheny was then. I still give the same answers I heard from him when I was 23.

As I pronounced the benediction, I finally exhaled. It was a good service. It was over.

Then, however, the funeral directors started the congregation up the aisles to file by the casket one last time, to have one last look at Danny's rouged yet pallid face, floating above the blue suit he'd never worn before. Old Brother Matheny stepped down and stood at the foot of the coffin. I followed his lead and stepped down and stood at the head.

School had been dismissed. All of Danny's classmates were there. The funeral directors started them up the aisle first. The girl at the head of the line looked at Danny and shrieked. The second girl screamed. The third girl moaned. They fell in a heap in front of Danny's coffin, weeping and wailing and gnashing their teeth, fell on top of one another, Sunday dresses all askew, beating their fists upon the floor and upon the bodies of those who had fallen with them. The comfort in the words of Old Brother Matheny had lasted less than five minutes.

Others took up the cry. Danny's teammates fainted in the aisles. The entire congregation began to wail and to moan. The white frame church building began to shake. I could feel the anger and the fear and the dismay coming up through my feet and into my legs until I trembled, not so much from fear, but just because the ground upon which I stood was no longer the bedrock of an American village. This ground was suddenly the precipice of the slippery slope to what the Psalmists call simply "the pit."

I looked around me for some symbol of sanity. The school teachers and church elders were moaning and rocking along with the housewives and farmers. The undertakers stood at the rear of the church, in each others arms, crying. Old Brother Matheny was slumped over the foot of the coffin, beating on it with his fist, weeping.

Danny's father got up from his pew and made his way up to me, stepping on the pile of girls as he came. He explained that it was time for him to take Danny home. He started to pull the body from the coffin.

In the crowd I saw my new wife, a year younger than I, still a college student, sitting rigid and still. Her eyes were moist, but the light of reality was in them. Not for the last time, in the sanity of those eyes I saw strength that I could use.

I wrestled Danny's body away from his father and shoved it back into the coffin. I hugged Danny's father close against my skinny chest and pulled him back to his pew. I closed the coffin lid and used the little handle, like a miniature crank for an old car, to seal it shut. I dragged the writhing girls out of the middle aisle. I pulled Old Brother Matheny off the coffin and sat him on the edge of the little chancel. I pushed the coffin down the aisle to the doors and there made the undertakers help me carry it out to the hearse.

By this time the building had stopped shaking. A layer of old shrieks and moans, now as quiet as someone else's memories, drooped pale and still just above our heads. Sullenly, people emerged from the church, not together, just individuals, their eyes fixed upon the few inches of ground just before their feet.

I gathered up my wife. We got into our stubby yellow English Ford. We led the long black hearse to the graveyard, two twisting miles east of town. No one had plowed the snow from the roads in the cemetery. We drove in anyway. There were many cars in the procession, but not many people emerged from them as I stood beside the coffin and committed the body to its resting place.

Helen and I left my three churches at the end of May. She had completed her college degree. I was headed for Perkins School of Theology at Southern Methodist University to learn how to be a minister.

From February to June, people came to worship, but there were no special events, no potlucks, no hymn sings. People were polite, but no one invited the young minister and his new wife to a meal. They couldn't forgive us.

"the south
ⓢhall rise again."

It was 1960, the year I first voted. The presidential election featured John F. Kennedy, a senator from Massachusetts, and Richard M. Nixon, the incumbent Vice President.

I should have voted for Nixon, of course. True, he was from California, which made him suspect, but he had been selected for the Vice Presidency by the quintessential midwesterner, the man from Kansas, the hero of our childhood years, Dwight D. Eisenhower. And he was Protestant.

Kennedy was obviously not the correct choice. He was Roman Catholic, and Protestants from Indiana knew that Catholics wanted to take over the school system. We further knew that a Catholic president would have to take orders from the pope, whose first order would probably be a ban on all Friday meat sales, favoring New England fishermen and hurting the Midwest's beef economy. To make things worse, Kennedy said "Cuber" when he should have said "Cuba."

Protestants, however, hold responsibility in high esteem. We tend to divide the world into two camps: those who take responsibility and those who don't. John F. Kennedy took responsibility, and he preached it. Helen and I heard our own voice in his campaign idealism. "Ask not what your country can do for you, but ask what you can do for your country."[1] We gladly cast our first presidential ballots for him. We wanted our unborn children to grow up in his kind of world.

It was 1960, the year that I went to seminary at the Perkins School of Theology at Southern Methodist University. I had dreamed about seminary and planned for it ever since I had answered the call to ministry. I had written every seminary in the country for catalogs, then pored over those catalogs, selected courses that intrigued me, compared tuitions, read the descriptions of what it would be like to live in Boston or New Haven or Atlanta.

I had intended to go to the school of theology at Boston University. That's where my hero, Bishop Richard Raines, had been educated. I was going to do my first year in Boston while Helen finished her senior year at Indiana University. Then we would be married. But the thought of separation proved too much for us. It always has. We decided to marry at the end of my senior year. I preached as a full-time lay pastor for a year while Helen finished her bachelor's degree. Then we went off to seminary together.

During that year, however, various of my older colleagues in ministry convinced me to go to Perkins. "That's where the cutting edge is," they said. "Boston is past its prime, and Drew is neo-orthodox, but Perkins has Albert Outler and Schubert Ogden and Van Harvey." I even heard Bishop Raines say, "If I were going to seminary today, I would choose Perkins." We went to Dallas.

We loaded up a rented trailer with our books and clothes and the furniture Helen's parents, "Tank" (Earl) and Georgia, had given us. I was just a little disgusted that they stood on the sidewalk and cried as they watched us drive away from their house in Gary, Indiana. Didn't they think I could take care of their daughter? Some 34 years later I watched our younger daughter, Kathleen, and her husband, Patrick, drive away in a rented truck to go to teach in Alabama. I was reasonably sure Patrick could take care of Katie. I knew Katie could take care of Patrick. But I stood on the sidewalk and cried.

In our Dallas year, 1960, Perkins was as advertised—exciting, theologically and socially. The faculty was superb, constantly challenging us to think new thoughts in new patterns. The students were mostly from the Southwest, but there were enough of the rest of us to challenge any stereotypes. Five hailed from Indiana. We were all pleased to be at the cutting-edge seminary.

Part of the cutting edge was in race relations. Perkins was the only college of Southern Methodist University that admitted Negro students. We had only two or three, but that was enough for most of Dallas, including the major newspapers, to apply the word "Communist" to Perkins on a regular basis.

It was 1960, the year that the civil rights movement was aborning in Dallas. Several of the Perkins students ate regularly at a lunch counter across the street from the campus. One day they took our Negro students with them. The owner called the pest control people. "There are some pests here I want to get rid of," he told them. The pest control people came and gladly sprayed the Perkins students, black and white, with pesticides, like roaches.

We were upset at the lack of concern for human life. DDT was still as common as chocolate, but everyone knew that spraying it on people wasn't going to be very good for them. We didn't fail to see the humor, though, or the ingenuity of the restaurant owner, in calling for pest control instead of for the police or the Klan.

One seminary administrator, a gentle and loving friend to all our students, thought there was nothing humorous about it, but not out of concern for human life. His concern was property. He argued quite seriously that the man had done the right thing, since property rights were paramount to all other rights. The owner was correct, he said, in taking whatever steps he thought were necessary to protect his business from those who were disrupting it.

Our administrator was not swayed by appeals to the rights of all citizens to eat in public places, the idea that Negroes should not be discriminated against because of the color of their skin, the fact that these were our fellow students, that Jesus loved everybody, or that the owner shouldn't be endangering health. Respect for property was the only thing that separated us from the Communists, he said, and that distinction from the Communists was the only thing that would allow us to continue as a Christian nation and not be swallowed up by godless Communism. When we pointed out that he seemed to have more faith in the power of godless Communists than in faithful Christians, he wasn't even fazed.

It was 1960, the year that Helen and I attended worship one Sunday morning at First Baptist Church in Dallas. The buildings covered what seemed to be a square block of downtown Dallas. The auditorium was huge. If I remember correctly, there were three balconies. We were seated in the second balcony.

We sang some hymns. The choir sang an anthem. The minister of Christian education plugged Reverend Criswell's latest book. Then Criswell rose to preach.

His theme seemed to be that John, who, as far as he was concerned, had written the Gospel of the same name, plus the Epistles of John, and Revelation, was an "age-ed" man. He certainly would have had to be an aged man had he written over that considerable time span.

"Age-ed" was his catch-word. Each time he came to it, he called out "age-ed" in a different way. He made us laugh, made us cry, made us hunch up to the front of our theater seats—all just by how he said "age-ed." About halfway through 30 minutes of this "age-ed" sermon, I stopped reacting and began to listen. The sermon really *was* about John being an aged man, nothing more, no other point. That didn't seem to bother anyone else, though. All the others in the auditorium continued to listen like school children (and teachers) listen for the last bell of the day. It was a magnificent demonstration of oratorical art, the ability to move a crowd, to raise it up or drop it low, to hold it in the palm of the hand, not by what was said, but simply by the way it was said.

At the end of the sermon Criswell called for those who wanted to respond to the fact that John was an "age-ed" man and to join the one true church—apparently meaning First Baptist—to come forward. To my amazement, about 20 persons did so. He asked each their name and where they were from. He announced the names to the congregation and welcomed them to the fellowship of the church.

He came to the last couple in the line. They were from New Orleans. Their name was Saint.

It was 1960, the year of New Orleans school desegregation. A few Negro students had been admitted to a formerly all-white school. All the white parents had withdrawn their children in protest, except for one Methodist minister, who took his first-grade daughter to school there each day. I can still remember the pictures on our black and white television, the faces of middle-class white mothers twisted with rage, shouting obscenities, shaking their fists, straining to spit on that little girl, all because she was going to first grade, to learn to read and write, with little Negro children.

It was in that context that the Reverend Wally Amos Criswell, the spiritual leader of the largest white Baptist church in the land, put his hands on the heads of the Saints from New Orleans and, with eyes closed and head lifted toward the third balcony, prayed "for all the saints in New Orleans who are fighting for their rights and purity against the godless Communism foisted upon them by the demonic powers in Washington, D.C." Hands still on their heads, eyes still toward heaven, he pronounced the benediction, which I quote exactly: "By God, the South shall rise again. We ain't licked yet. Amen."

There was the barest moment of awe-struck silence. Then I heard an incredulous voice from the balcony. "By God, I'm from Detroit, and . . ."

We never heard what the man from Detroit was thinking. Maybe he was going to say, "That was the most inspiring thing I ever heard." Maybe he would have said, "That's the biggest pile of it I ever heard in church." But the organ swooped in with a mighty crash. Everyone was up, clattering seat backs, milling around, mostly smiling benignly.

Helen and I slipped out as quickly and as quietly as we could, hoping no one could tell from our looks that we were Yankees from that socially progressive state of Indiana, the only northern state ever to give George Wallace its vote, the only northern state ever to have an active Klan chapter in every county.

It was 1960, the year of the election, the year of Catholic John F. Kennedy and Texan Lyndon B. Johnson against Vice President Richard Nixon. It was the year that Lady Bird Johnson was spat on in the lobby of a Dallas hotel, the year that some Dallasite bopped Lyndon B., Texas' favorite son, on the head with a Richard Nixon campaign sign.

A friend read this story and said, "You can't blame all of Dallas for JFK's assassination." True, but still, even though I was shocked when I heard that John F. Kennedy had been shot, I was not surprised when I heard that it was in Dallas.

note

[1]A friend whom I won't name, just in case he's wrong, says he doesn't think this actual phrase was used in the campaign, but surfaced at the inauguration, as did its concerete applications, the Peace Corps and Alliance for Progress. The idea, however, was certainly there.

just ahead of
Albert Schweitzer

We had moved to Dallas in June, right after Helen graduated from IU, and I started to seminary immediately in summer school. Standing in the registration line, I heard a man introducing himself to another student.

"I'm Kenwood Bryant," he said.

Kenwood Bryant had been an Evansville schoolteacher and a part-time lay pastor when he preached at Forsythe. He used to come to the Forsythe community on Saturdays to visit "the flock." Sometimes he would come by our house and pick me up, to be his native guide on the backwoods gravel roads. Not knowing of my pact with God to save my sister's life, he encouraged me to consider entering the ministry. He had made a leap of faith, left his teaching job behind, and packed his family off to Dallas to go to seminary. I had not seen him or heard anything of him for several years. Now we were students together.

· · · · ·

Everything about Texas really *is* big, including the garbage truck in our neighborhood. It was a semi. Men walked along beside it and tossed cans up to other men who stood within it on the garbage. They dumped the garbage at their feet and tossed the cans back. Sometimes the walkers caught them, and sometimes they didn't bother. Other than utilities, garbage pickup was the only civic service in our part of town. We had no curbs, no gutters, no paved streets, no street lights.

One Saturday night Helen and I decided to go downtown to a movie. We had heard nothing about it, had read no reviews, but *Psycho* looked like it would be good, especially since it was what was playing. It started out well enough. When Janet Leigh stole the money from the office, a Dallas businessman down the row from us said in unbelieving tones, "Why, she's getting out of the real estate business!" That was the last laugh. Two hours later we staggered out of the theater, clutching each other in total fear, and drove back to our unlighted neighborhood on a moonless night.

When we got there, we found the yard light for our compound broken out and the gym door standing half open. We sat in our car outside the fence for what seemed like half the night, afraid to move, certain that Norman Bates was lurking in the dark just inside the gym. Finally, since we couldn't afford to spend the night in a motel and come back in the morning light, I got out and unlocked the gate and drove the car inside. With its headlights trained on the gym doors, I sneaked over, found the padlock on the ground, and quickly locked up, figuring if Norman were in there, he could just stay for a while. Later we learned that the Boy Scouts leader had lost control of the troop, not an unusual event, and it was the Scouts who had broken out the light. The leader, flustered, had forgotten to lock up properly. I still hope Norman will come back and get him for taking 10 years off my life.

· · · · ·

I made the mistake at Perkins of testing well on languages. There were three of us who tested high enough that we were put into an experimental program—taking both Hebrew and Greek instead of English Bible. We still had to pass the English Bible exams along with all the other students, however. To get us ready for that, at the end of each week our professors summarized in 30 minutes what the English Bible students had gotten all week to absorb.

Helen and I were in our second year of marriage and working full-time running a settlement house. Helen was running our household, and I was taking Greek and Hebrew along with the regular full load at Perkins. Together and separately we spoke to many church groups in a fairly successful effort to raise more funds for our program. We were dealing firsthand with racial segregation and homesickness. As the second semester started, we thought Helen was pregnant. Mrs. Merien catching us without the white rag on the gate was ostensibly what ended our time in Dallas, but it is doubtful we would have lasted three years under that kind of pressure.

We had wonderful friends there, though—Doug and Helen Gatton, who had gone to Indiana State University in Terre Haute; Bob Kochtitzky, from Mississippi; Bob Parsons, who was already a good friend from the Wesley Foundation at Indiana University, and who lived with us for a month when he came late to school; Harold and Thelma Reynolds; Jimmy and Ann Jones; Woodie Smith.

What a thrill it was to study with Albert Outler, Schubert Ogdon, Van Harvey, Herndon Wagers, Franklin Littell, Victor Furnish, William Farmer, H. Grady Hardin, Claude Evans, W. J. A. Power, Douglas Jackson, and Dean Joseph Quillian.

Helen learned to make pizza and then cut my hair while we watched "Bonanza" on Saturday nights. We had our first pets there, two goldfish named "Funny" and "Flippy."

It was a stressful year, but so full that we probably remember more from those quick months than any other period of our lives.

• • • • •

We were invited to talk to the youth group at a large suburban church where Jimmy Jones was youth minister. Apparently, the members were impressed. They raised funds for us and did volunteer work at Rankin. Later in the year, when Jimmy asked them to name the greatest Christians they knew, we came in first, just ahead of Albert Schweitzer!

• • • • •

Dallas was *hot!* We went Christmas shopping in short sleeves. We bought a small air conditioning unit for our "upstairs" room, where I studied, and there wasn't a single month, not even January, when we didn't use it at least one day. Our only cooler for the downstairs, however, was a "water fan," an interesting contraption that is exactly what its name says—a fan that blows over water and pushes the hydrated and presumably cooler air from the outside into the house. We used it a lot. The problem was that it mildewed everything, including our clothes and shoes in the closet. In a neighborhood with dirt streets, you can't even leave the windows open for cooling without taking the dust along with the air. We asked the board about getting an air conditioner for downstairs, but Mrs. Merien said there was no money for "frills," and that we'd get used to the heat "once your blood thins."

One day Mrs. *Gilmore, the president of the board, telephoned to inform us that the board would hold its next meeting at our house. She didn't ask, just set the date and time and told us to be there to let them in. We unplugged the water fan and stored up heat for a week. The board members arrived in their hats and silk dresses and sensible shoes—and probably corsets and nylon slips, although I cannot attest to them—and took their places in our Saharan living room. They started "glowing" before the minutes from the last meeting were over.

"My goodness," said Mrs. Gilmore, "why isn't the water fan on?"

"Oh, it's not working," I said, "It'll get better when our blood thins out."

I'm sure it was the shortest meeting the board ever had.

The next day an air conditioning unit was delivered to our house. It was so big, I had to get Fernando and Charlie Adams, the custodian, to help me get it into the window. We stayed cool, even in January.

for Pete'ⓢ sake

Rankin Community Center had a fence all around the grounds, around the gym and the nursery school building and the playground and the library and the sewing rooms and the courtyard and the woodshop and the director's house, where we lived. It was a good, high, sturdy fence. It was a necessary fence, because it was a dangerous neighborhood, at least dangerous for 1960. If you could plunk that same neighborhood down anywhere 40 years later, it would seem quite safe.

We opened up the gate to let people in—children for the nursery school or Mary Lou Avila's afterschool activities, teens for Don Post's athletic program or weekend dances, women for Helen's sewing classes, middle-aged adults for the evening English and citizenship classes, Boy Scouts, open houses. Once everyone was inside, however, the gates were locked again until it was time to leave.

Pete had never been inside the fence. I watched him from the window of my house. I had been watching him since Sunday, almost a week now, from inside the fence, from behind my window. He had come each day, haunting me with his vacant eyes and dirty face and ripped t-shirt, the same shirt every day. He just stood there, staring at the locked gate.

Finally, I left my house and went to the fence. I asked him if he wanted to come in. He hesitated, then nodded his head. I opened the gates just a little bit. Pete slipped by me. He was in.

I was young. I hadn't made any really big mistakes before. Pete aged me quickly in that regard, and in some others, too.

Once inside, Pete lost all shyness. He started fights. He climbed into the gym's balcony and dropped roller skates on the children below. He punched holes in the basketballs. He wrote on the walls. He tore down the swings. He was a disease, but I didn't have a cure.

I tried to talk with him, tried to learn what demon was driving him, so that we might exorcise it with love or discipline or bran, but Pete didn't talk. So I walked the dusty streets of the neighborhood, talking to others about Pete, asking people what they knew about our bad boy. Pete didn't talk, but the neighbors were willing to talk about him. There were many children in his family. No one knew exactly how many, but a conservative estimate was nine. He had an older brother who was a gangster. There had been a succession of fathers in the home, and almost all the children bore different last names. Pete had a baby sister whom he hated, and whom he had twice attempted to kill.

I walked back home at the sag end of the day, wanting to be there when the gates were open to let the nursery school children out and the afterschool children in. As I dragged through the dust, I decided Pete didn't have the proverbial two strikes against him. At the age of 10 he had already struck out. He was far beyond anything we could do for him. Being inside would do him no good, and might well do the rest of us a great deal of harm. I decided Pete would have to go—back outside the fence.

Fernando Torres asked for a chance with him. Fernando was a neighborhood man, often unemployed, now a part-time teacher for us.

"Let me have him in woodshop," he said.

"Fernando, you're a brave man, but I'm not willing to let that boy have a hammer or saw in his hand when other children are around."

"So, we'll have a class of one," said Fernando.

The woodshop was the only building in the center, other than our house, that had a direct door to the outside. Pete didn't have to come inside the fence. I didn't even have to see him. I agreed to let Fernando take him on as long as he used the outside door. I didn't like to think about problems I couldn't solve, people I couldn't help, 10-year-olds already in the world's scrap heap with no chance of getting out. I still don't. I gladly agreed with myself to forget about Pete.

Christmas is a bad time in a neighborhood center. So many requests for food and fuel and other sorts of help come in every day, and the resources never stretch far enough. I'd finally put Pete on a back shelf of my mind and our buildings, but Christmas was twisting the worry faucet again.

Of course, who should appear at my back door right then but Pete himself, eyes flashing. I silently cursed whoever had left the gate open, hoping it wasn't me. He held several pieces of wood, which were more or less fastened together. Fernando was a good man, but I got the impression he wasn't a very good shop teacher. I stared. Pete spoke.

"It's a cradle, Mister John. It's a Christmas present for my baby sister."

We talked awhile, Pete and I, standing there at my back door, finally sitting down side by side on the steps. We talked about carpentry and babies and Christmas. Then Pete went back outside the fence, went home, bearing his Christmas present, a star in his eyes. I went out into the neighborhood, too, distributing Christmas presents. I left the gate open behind me.

We saw no more of the angry boy who had first slipped inside the fence. Another little boy came in his place. His name was Pete, but we barely recognized him. I still do not know just what Fernando, that inept carpenter, had done with him. Nor do I know what became of Pete after we left Dallas, only a few months later. I like to think that somewhere he's teaching a lost-cause woodshop class.

ⓐ white rag on
the gate

I was looking out the kitchen window of our house, inside the fence that surrounded our buildings and yards, watching for Don, our football coach. If he showed up for practice, it would be the first time all week. If he didn't show, I'd have to practice the kids again myself. When you're the director of a settlement house, you do anything that has to be done. But I hadn't been a high school footballer, and my football knowledge was pretty well used up. Don had played in college. He was a Perkins student, too. I needed him there, so I watched for him, as though looking closely at the place where he should be would make him appear.

Instead, I saw the powder blue Cadillac turn the corner and ooze up to our gate. Good grief; Mrs. *Merien at the worst possible time!

The white rag wasn't tied to the gate. Helen was in the sewing room, getting ready for a dozen little girls. She wouldn't even know Mrs. Merien was there. I couldn't get the rag onto the gate myself with Mrs. Merien parked beside it. My best hope was to get her into the living room of our house, where she couldn't see the courtyard, and hope that Don came to work.

The Cadillac's door swung open, and Mrs. Merien emerged in her usual outfit—expensive silk dress over black and white saddle shoes. I had once spoken to a women's group from her church at her home in Highland Park. The living room was so long that there was a piano in either end of it. Old Negro men in short white coats served lunch to more than a hundred women in hats, seated by fours at tables around the room. The tables had the look of being there on a permanent basis.

I dashed out our kitchen door and unlocked the gate for her. She headed for the trunk of her car.

"I got a special deal on garbage cans, so I brought you one."

The treasurer of the board of directors of Rankin Community Center was not a woman to shirk the details.

I grabbed the can, got it and Mrs. Merien inside the fence, and started to relock the gate.

"Won't the children be coming?" she asked.

Well, of course, they would. School was out. They'd be there for Fernando's woodshop class, and Helen's sewing class, and Mr. Reinhardt's English literacy class, and Mary Lou Avila's game time. They'd be there for football practice. Mrs. Franco and Edna Mae and Teresa would be sending the little children home from nursery school. I couldn't lock the gate because kids would be piling up on both sides of it. There would be some on the outside that I didn't dare let Mrs. Merien see.

"Oh, right. Just force of habit."

I reluctantly left the gate half open, trying to think up a reason I could give her for tying my white handkerchief into its mesh. There was none.

I got her into the kitchen, but she wouldn't budge beyond it. As we stood there talking Rankin Community Center business, I did the best I could to keep my slender frame between her and the glass of the back door.

The knock came. I kept on talking. It came again, louder this time. Mrs. Merien looked puzzled.

"Aren't you going to answer that?"

"No need, really. Just kids. They'll find their way."

She stepped around me and pulled the door open. There was Marcus, our quarterback.

"Mr. John, Don's not here. Should I pass out the equipment?"

Then the eyes in his round, brown face got very big. The eyes in Mrs. Merien's round white face got very small.

"Who are you?"

"Uh, I'm Marcus." He didn't know what else to say, except to add "M'am."

She rotated on her saddle shoes toward me. "What's he doing here?"

When the board hired me as the Director of Rankin Community Center, and Helen as a program worker, they made it clear that "Nigras" were not to be allowed into the center or its programs, even though they made up about a third of the community we served. This was done in a gentle way, by genteel ladies, pointing out that it was not practical to let Negroes into our programs since there was a "language problem." We were unsure what the language problem was, since half of the people we served used a language—Spanish—that we neither spoke nor understood, and the Negroes spoke English, with the same accent used by the white children and parents who came to the center.

I hadn't known many Negroes in my life. Mrs. Dickerson lived next door to us in Indianapolis, where we had moved when I was four and where we lived until I was 10. There were no other Negroes in our entire neighborhood, though. Sometimes Mrs. Dickerson would give me a nickel for running an errand for her, but she was old, and we didn't see her outside very much. There was one elderly Negro couple in Oakland City. I'd see them working in their garden in the spring when the school bus passed their house.

At Indiana University there were Negro boys in my dorm, Linden Hall East, the AHAYWEHs.[1] I respected Stan Cox and Dick Bennett, nice guys, excellent scholars, fellow AHAYWEHs. The one I was closest to, though, was Tom Atkins, who became I.U.'s first Negro student body president, later the first black to be elected to the Boston City Council. Helen and I visited him in Boston after we had all graduated. He took me to a black power rally, the only white person there. He's had a distinguished career as a civil rights lawyer. I.U. named an African-American living/learning center for him.

I had been taught, both by my mother and by Forsythe Church, that God was color-blind. I was quite sure I was, too.

Shortly after we moved to Dallas, I had to take our car to a service station for repair. I drove over to one of the main roads and stopped at the first station that displayed the brand of my one credit card. A large Negro man walked out of the station. I had never done business with a Negro person before, only seen them from a distance or lived with them in a dorm. The first thought that flashed through my mind was, "I'm going to get cheated."

The second thought was, "I'm as prejudiced as all the prejudiced people I so despise for their prejudice." Being poor and righteous gives one the moral high ground over the rich and unrighteous, like the genteel ladies of the Rankin board. It looked as if our only difference was financial, not moral. It was not a good thought.

During football season we fielded a team in the city recreation league. After an especially devastating loss, some of the Mexican kids came to me and said, "Mr. John, we're getting the ____ beat out of us in this league. We're too little. We need some of the big Negro boys from around here on our team. We've talked to them. They're willing to play. How come they can't be on the team?"

I talked to Don, our football coach. He had played collegiately at New Mexico State. The board was the only reason we could think of to keep those boys off the team.

"Do any board members ever come to the games?" I asked.

"Are you kidding?" said Don.

The next week our team started winning. I reported that at a board meeting. The ladies were pleased.

Once the big Negro boys were on the football team, their little brothers and sisters wanted to know why they couldn't come inside the fence—to sewing class or woodshop or roller skating parties in our gym. Their parents wanted to come inside the fence, too—to enroll their children in our nursery school or come to GED classes or the women's homemaking courses. The other teens wanted to come inside the fence—to Friday night recreation or to play basketball. We agreed to let them inside the fence, provided they stayed outside when there was a white rag tied to the gate.

Inside the high wire fence were our house, the courtyard, the gym, the nursery school, the play yard, the woodshop, the library, and the classrooms. Inside our fence was the action for the neighborhood around Crossman Avenue. Inside our fence was the place to be.

One Saturday night the first week or two we lived there, we parked our car outside the fence to make room in the courtyard for the teen dance. Some boys came late. Our rules, of necessity, were strict: You had to be there before the gate was closed; and once you left, you were gone for the night. I refused to let them in. They claimed, in the manner of teens everywhere, that they had always been let in late by my predecessor. I stood firm.

When the dance was over, I moved my car back inside the fence. Someone had taken a key and gashed the beautiful mint green paint of my six-month-old car, from front to rear several times. It wasn't much of a car—no chrome, no white walls, no air conditioning, no automatic transmission or radio or power steering or power brakes. The cheapest Plymouth with the smallest engine ever made. We were lucky it had seats. But it was the first new car I'd ever had. It had the prettiest paint job I'd ever seen. I was heartbroken.

The next Friday night I again parked the car outside the fence, and the latecomers were again turned away. If you wanted inside, with the action, you had to live by the rules. We wouldn't be intimidated. Being inside was too important to those kids for them to take any more chances. We had no more latecomers. Nothing more happened to our car.

If it were that important to the Mexican kids and the Anglo kids to be inside, then it was that important to the Negro kids, too. Now Mrs. Merien was inside, watching that polyglot of kids streaming through the gate—black and brown and white.

"I think there's been a mistake," she said. I thought so, too, but I suspected we had two different mistakes in mind. My mistake cost us our jobs and sent us back to Indiana.

My successor at Rankin wrote to say that there was no longer a need for the white rag on the gate. The Negro children kept coming to the center, and no one tried to stop them.

We couldn't remain in seminary without jobs, so we returned to Indiana. My old college friend, Bill C. Brown, gave me a job selling life insurance in his agency. I figured my career in ministry was over. We were going to have a child before long. I had to earn a living. It seemed a strange way to learn that my strange call had not been real after all.

note

[1]A sobriquet taken from Dante, "Abandon Hope All Ye Who Enter Here."

the death of the president—and of God

Yes, that flash photo is still in my mind, in black and white. The picture of where I was when I learned that President Kennedy had been shot—the Garrett Theological Seminary cafeteria.

Without our jobs at Rankin Community Center, we could not afford to stay in school at Perkins. We left Dallas and returned to Indiana. I sojourned for a while in the far country of selling life insurance, unsure whether or not I wanted to pastor a church that was not open to people of all races. But the memory of my call was too strong. When I needed to be reading insurance manuals, I caught myself reading books about pastoring.

Bishop Richard Raines, always a mentor and protector to me, gave me a student appointment to the Methodist church in Cedar Lake, Indiana, about 15 miles south of Gary. I transferred from Perkins to Garrett, at Northwestern University, and commenced three years of a 140-mile daily round-trip commute to Evanston, Illinois, before the days of interstate highways, through Chicago. The drive took four to six hours per day, according to the volume of the traffic and the interest level of my car.

I studied at Garrett from 1961 to 1964. Those years were the numerical high-water mark of mainline Protestantism in America. People came into churches by the dozens. The Cedar Lake church received 103 new members the first year I was there, increasing its size by a third. I took it for granted. Just a regular year. In all the rest of my ministry I never received that many new members in one year, even in a city where my church had a thousand members. Indeed, since 1964, the year I graduated from Garrett, my denomination and others like it have suffered numerical decline every year. I can only hope that my ascent to ordained and full-time pastoral status and the numerical decline of American Protestantism are merely coincidental!

Professor Henry Kolbe was filling in for Professor Richard Ford as the director of scholarships at the time. He welcomed me to Garrett by saying, "You're the first transfer student to whom we've ever given a scholarship, and I don't think you should have one either!" I have no idea who the other members of the scholarship committee were, but I've always been thankful to them for overriding the irascible Henry, which probably gave them all much secret pleasure.

Bruce Johnson was the first student I met at Garrett. He saw me wandering lost in the hallways and took the trouble to welcome me. We remained friends until he and his wife, Eugenia, were murdered in their parsonage in Chicago, a crime that remains unsolved after almost 30 years. When I received my doctorate, we had a celebration in the Hoopeston, Illinois, church where I was serving. On the bulletin I dedicated that service to the Johnsons and to Mary Albers, an Illinois State University Wesley Foundation student who died of cancer at the age of 24 while in the Peace Corps in the Philippines.

I was eating lunch in the Garrett cafeteria with Bruce when something pulled our attention through the glass walls into the lounge. Everyone there was standing and staring open-mouthed at various parts of the ceiling. I dipped my head to see if the second floor was making a descent, but the building seemed intact.

Then fellow student Ed Tucker hurried into the cafeteria.

"Kennedy's been shot," he gasped.

I realized those in the lounge had been pulled to their feet by such incredible words, to stare in this early age of television at the radio speakers from which such impossible news poured forth.

Bruce and I left our lunch and went into the lounge with the others, to take our places, staring up, shocked by the enormity of the occasion, but having no idea that the Protestant church and the Protestant ministry had been changed forever by the death of the Catholic president.

I had answered the call to ministry with the full intent of changing the world. John F. Kennedy assumed the presidency with the same premise: "Ask not what your country can do for you, but ask what you can do for your country." I was sure that he and Helen and I together, along with Bruce and Eugenia and Ed and Donna and Tom and Sally and so many other young people of high ideals, could change not just the country but the world. We would bring an end to racial and religious division, poverty, war, and injustice. Well, perhaps not bring an end to those evil powers, but reduce them to minor players on the world scene.

When Kennedy was murdered in Dallas, those hopes began to melt like ice cubes when the party's over. We held onto the ideals for a while, but America started to change from hope to cynicism, from service to greed, from civility to violence. Certainly, cynicism and violence and greed had always been there. H. Rap Brown claimed that "violence is as American as cherry pie." Now, though, in the death of Kennedy, cynicism, violence, and greed gained critical mass. They started to become the norm rather than the exception. Our motto increasingly became, "Ask only what you can get for yourself."

The world changed, and so did the church. So did the ministry. I had answered the call of both God and John F. Kennedy. One of them was now dead. Very soon, they would begin to claim the other one was, too.

publish or parish

My friend Jack Newsome tells the story of the uneducated, backwoods preacher who was preaching from an Old Testament story about a man called Naaman. The preacher couldn't read, but he had heard the story many times, a story ostensibly about how Naaman was healed of his leprosy by the prophet Elisha.[1] In the King James Version of the story, Naaman, a military man, is described as "a mighty man in valor, but he was a leper." The preacher had heard some of the words of the story through his own filter, so he preached mightily about "Naaman the leaper, a mighty man of value." His imagination got the best of him, and it turned out that Naaman could leap over almost anything. That was what made him of such value to the army, since he could leap over the walls of any city and then open the gates for his men to come in and conquer.

It was a great and powerful sermon, a mighty sermon of value. Afterwards, however, one of his listeners said to him, "You know, the story actually says that Naaman was a leper instead of a leaper, and a man of valor rather than a man of value."

The preacher huffed, "Are you going to ruin a perfectly good sermon over two little words?"

Well, yes. Most of the church has always felt that those little distinctions between leper and leaper and valor and value make a difference. Consequently, we want our ministers to be educated. The first college established in America, Harvard, was set there in the middle of Cambridge precisely so Americans would have an educated clergy. A minister should feel that she or he is called by God to be a minister, but call is not enough. Affirmation of the call by the church is necessary, but such affirmation is not enough. Education is necessary, too. We need to know the difference between leper and leaper. The first three written accounts of Jesus' life and teachings all report that he said we should love God with our minds as well as our hearts and souls and strength.[2] If we are to do that, we need leaders with educated, disciplined minds.

To that end, not only Harvard but also most of the other great historic universities were established first to educate clergy, and almost every denomination has established its own theological schools, also called seminaries, for the education of ministers. There is an increasing number of nondenominational, independent seminaries. Almost everyone, it seems, wants to ensure an educated clergy.

Garrett Theological Seminary[3] was on the campus of Northwestern University, originally a Methodist school, in Evanston, Illinois, just north of Chicago. In 1968, the Methodist Church and the Evangelical United Brethren (EUB) Church united to form the United Methodist Church. The EUBs had a seminary, Evangelical, at Naperville, Illinois, south of Chicago. It seemed reasonable to unite the seminaries of the two denominations along with the denominations themselves. Thus, Evangelical Seminary moved up to Evanston, and the two became one, Garrett-Evangelical, on the Garrett campus. I graduated from Garrett, before the union, in 1964.

In 1989, I returned to Garrett-Evangelical for my class's 25th-year reunion. Only a handful of my classmates joined me there. A few more wrote a brief note for the booklet the seminary put together for the occasion. Most just ignored our silver anniversary.

I've wondered a good deal about that. Had they simply lost touch with the school? Were they all just too busy? Did they not want to face classmates who smelled too strongly of greater "success"? Was it because most of the professors we remembered were no longer there? Were they embarrassed to return? 1964, after all, was the end of Methodist triumphalism, the first year of "decline," when the denomination began to mourn a net membership loss each year. We are the class of educated ministers, more than any other, that has presided over that decline.

I think, however, that the absence of my classmates was due to something beyond busyness, embarrassment, and the absence of beloved and ridiculed professors. I fear that few seminary graduates of our era believe that our education has much continuity with who we are and what we do now.

When the seminary umbilical cord was cut in May of 1964, we educated newborns were carried out to the curb on Sheridan Road and tossed into the cars of passing strangers. We had been warned by our professors how that once they had us in their cars, the strangers would drive us to distraction. They would take up our time with mundane matters, keep us from our studies, make us into pastors instead of scholars, psychologists, or chaplains. They might, we were warned, even try to be colleagues and friends instead of clients and members.

That was the basic break: Our education's form, especially, but also its content, prepared us for the old, hierarchical church, not for the new, horizontal, laity-beating-at-the-sacristy-door church. We were educated to be caretaking pastoral counselors rather than evangelistic, democratic leaders. Our education became irrelevant to the work we do.

Neither the parish nor the parish ministry was respected by most other theologically trained professionals. As we graduated, and for several years thereafter, some theologians and other scholars of religion actually began to predict the end of the congregation. The old was to be replaced with new forms of communal church life, although those were rarely spelled out in detail.[4] The congregation would just wither away, they predicted. The absence of respect for the parish also influenced how we were taught and what we learned.

Most of us were already serving as student pastors, so we did not see other pastors at work. Our teachers were

scholars, not pastors. We never saw a faculty member conduct a wedding or a funeral or make a hospital call. We saw
them stand up and lecture. They were our models and our
teachers, even though they were not modeling pastoral ministry. When they tried to *teach* us what we should do as
pastors, they only reinforced what they modeled.

This type of teaching occurred in an academic and clois-
tered setting, a Christian community devoid of laity. The
laypeople we encountered on the weekends were merely
examples we would use as we learned from one another in
the real Christian community, the Protestant monastery, the
seminary. We were not educated to aid the priesthood of
believers. We were the professionals; church members were
our students or clients, just as professors, hospital chaplains,
and psychologists had students or clients.

The rise of spiritual and political democracy made the
hierarchical preaching and ministry methods in which we
were educated obsolete.

The pastoral counseling movement was in full flower in
the mainline churches in the early 1960s. Carroll Wise, one
of my professors, was one of its chief proponents. "Human
help for human hurt," Wise called it. Ministers were to spend
their time with parishioners one-on-one, as doctors and
psychologists did. We were not to teach or evangelize, but to
listen and reflect. Certainly we should not confuse a counse-
lee by inviting her to join the church; she might think we
were trying to build up the institution instead of listening to
her pain. No one thought to question the strength of being a
part of the worshiping and serving congregation, if such
participation might not be therapeutic, and if we weren't
shortchanging people who came to us in their need if we did
not offer them the human help of the whole congregation
instead of the pastor only.

Clinical Pastoral Education (CPE), the laboratory arm of
the pastoral counseling movement, is practical. Students
serve full-time, usually for a quarter or a semester, in an

institutional setting, usually a general or mental hospital, under the supervision of a chaplain or professor who is certified for the job. Students work with patients, then write up their "cases" and present them for critique in group session to the supervisor and other students. Ideally, a student learns not just about techniques, but about him/herself. It's a good and useful program. It is, however, mostly irrelevant to the parish.

I did parish-based CPE 10 years after seminary. The participants were pastors who remained in their parish work and met one day a week with a professor at a university hospital. We used case studies from our parishes. I later mentioned my experience to a hospital chaplain and CPE supervisor who snorted, "You can't do decent CPE that way. You've got to be under supervision in a hospital. You shouldn't even get credit for parish-based CPE." He was probably right about the credit, but for the wrong reason. The pastoral counseling movement and CPE are discontinuous with parish ministry.

In seminary the professors warned students that the parish would be unlike the seminary. They were right. I don't remember that a single moment of even one seminary class was devoted to how to make a hospital call or conduct a funeral or deal with the bride's mother at a wedding rehearsal or keep the trustees from thinking they are the finance committee; 100% of my seminary education prepared me very well for 20% of what I have done in ministry.

Some seminary educators say that is the way it should be, that the proper role of the theological school is to give people the tools by which they can dig into the soil of the parish for themselves, not to teach them techniques or skills. It is, in other words, a theological school, not a trade school. Perhaps they are right. But a great deal of grief could be saved for both ministers and congregations if someone would just explain about the church officer who begs to be let out of her job and then tells everyone you pushed her out, or how to personalize a funeral, or the difference between a choir director and an Arab terrorist.[5]

Both our faculty and student body understood that the bright folks went on to graduate work, and thus college or seminary teaching, or became CPE supervisors or campus ministers or went into some other "special appointment." The attitude was that if you couldn't get anything else, you went to the parish. There was a constant joking takeoff on the professors' lament that it was "publish or perish." Among the students it was "publish (a Ph.D. dissertation) or parish."

Those in the "hard" disciplines looked down upon the "practical" fields, and even on the teachers in those fields, especially if they did not have the right jots and tittles following their names. Most seminaries would rather hire as a professor of preaching or parish ministry someone who holds a Ph.D. in medieval history from a foreign university rather than someone who's spent 20 years doing the weekly preaching and parish work for which students need to be prepared. Despite rhetoric to the contrary, most seminary professors are "of" the academy, even though they may be "in" the church.

Parish ministers are seen by seminaries and church bureaucrats as consumers. In most journals or conferences for parish ministers, not half of the articles or workshops are written or conducted by parish ministers. Usually, none of them are. Apparently, the only requirement for teaching parish ministers is not to be one. Certainly, parish ministers are never asked to write for journals or to present papers or workshops at conferences for professors or chaplains. The assumption, denied on every hand but practiced consistently, is that parish ministers know little about anything, including their own profession. Not only do they have nothing to contribute to those in other professions, they don't even have anything worthwhile to share with their peers. That is not what the seminary professes, but it is what we were taught, and it continues to be the standard.

I was educated for the wrong church, by the wrong people, to do the wrong work, in the wrong profession. I loved every minute of it—the widening horizons, the mental challenge, the fellowship of students and professors, the sense of belonging to "the goodly fellowship of the prophets" from the faith's first moment up to the present. I recall my wrong education, and my wrong educators, with great affection.

notes

[1]You can read about this for yourself in 2 Kings 5.

[2]Mark 12:30; Matthew 22:37; Luke 10:27.

[3]It was established by Eliza Garrett in memory of her husband, the first mayor of Chicago, and was originally called Garrett Biblical Institute.

[4]Mentioned were communes; coffeehouses; base-church units such as the early Wesleyan cell groups and those that exist in Latin America today; Bible study groups; industrial missions; house churches; laity attached to monastic orders; laity components of theological schools; and para-church groups such as those on college campuses, for example, Navigators, IV, and Campus Crusade.

[5]Preacher joke: The difference between a choir director and an Arab terrorist is that you can negotiate with an Arab terrorist.

birthing daughter⑤
—and burying them

"Can you do me a favor?"

Mel's voice was a little higher than usual. Maybe it was just telephone distortion, but I didn't think so. Besides, ministers know that "Can you do me a favor?" isn't a question; it's just a warning. I'd been preaching for only five years, but I knew that.

"There's this family that lives over here near me. You don't know them. They don't come to our church. They don't go anywhere to church. I don't even know them that well, but . . . their little girl got killed last night. Only 14. Slipped out of the house late and went out riding in a car with some boy who'd been drinking at one of the taverns. It was after midnight, and he's only 16, but you know how they stay open for hours after the legal closing time. They'll serve anybody; all the kids know that. Anyway, he crashed the car, and *Jill . . . she was killed . . . a whole bunch of kids in the car, and nobody else even hurt too bad . . . but she was dead . . ."

"Do they want me to do a funeral, Mel?"

"Probably. I've talked with the dad a little. They don't have anybody else to do it. But, uh, that's not exactly the real problem right now. Her mother, well, *April, she's acting like nothing's wrong, saying Jill's just off for a little visit and she'll be back soon. *Jeff, her husband, and the rest of the family, and even me . . . God, the funeral director's been there even . . . she won't listen to anybody . . . It's so weird, her acting like everything's hunkie-dorie and everybody else sitting around crying and making funeral plans . . ."

Was this what God had called me to, a lifetime of dead children and denying parents and grieving friends? I'd been through a year of seminary, but I still didn't know what to do, anymore than I had with Billy Quick or with Danny.

My own daughter was not much more than a year old. Mary Beth had been born the day I took my entrance exams at Garrett Theological Seminary. Helen felt some pains before I pulled out of the church's gravel parking lot behind our house that morning to drive the 70 miles from Cedar Lake, Indiana, to Evanston, Illinois—before interstate highways, across country roads, up the Calumet Expressway, 93rd Street over to the Outer Drive, finally winding through a dozen different streets along the lake to the Northwestern University campus in Evanston.

I completed my exams in record time and headed home. Helen had already started for the hospital in Hammond, 20 miles away. Len Deters, our neighbor, had her in his old Chevy when they met me on the county line road south of Crown Point. I was driving with a purpose, looking neither to left nor right, but they saw me flash by. Len's horn wouldn't work. He turned around and pursued me almost all the way back to Cedar Lake before he got my attention, and we got Helen transferred to our car so I could take her to St. Margaret's.

There were problems in the aftermath of delivery. I didn't get to hold my new daughter until she was two weeks old. When the nurse brought Helen and Mary Beth to the car, I just grabbed that baby and held her in my arms until the cops made me get in the car and leave.

Now Mary Beth would bounce and sway whenever she heard "Baby Elephant Walk" on the radio. Her face would light up, and she would say "Hi, Da," whenever I came home. Could I deal with it, if 13 years from now she came home dead some night? Would our pastor, whoever might be hauled into that role for the occasion, have anything to say or do to make it better?

It's one of those things that wears you down in the ministry. Every time a grief comes to someone else, you not only deal with their loss but with the anticipation of your own. At 24 I didn't know how much that would grind me down by the time I was 34, and 44, and 54 . . .

Another thing that wears you down: people really want you to have magical powers. Jesus brought Jairus' daughter back from the dead. Why shouldn't one whom Jesus has called do the same? Or at least, shouldn't a pastor have something "magical" to say that will make it acceptable? In this case, to make it acceptable literally, to make that mother accept the fact that her child was dead.

People don't call the letter carrier, or the schoolteacher, or the factory worker, or the editor at a time like this. Most of the time they don't even bother with the psychologist. They know psychologists don't have the power anymore than letter carriers have the power. Ministers don't have the power, either, but folks don't want to believe that, not when they need the power so much. They want the minister. They want the minister now. They want the minister to say the words of power, make the signs of power, do the mighty acts of power.

Church members usually know we don't have the power. They've been around us long enough to know us and our weaknesses. They've been around God long enough to know that love is more important than power. Church members know that ministers have little power, but we have some love we can share. That love has been planted and watered and cultivated over a growing season or two with them. Church members don't expect magic. They just expect us to be there.

Those outside the church think we have some special line to the Almighty, that we can pull that string on their behalf if we choose. Sometimes they get very angry when we don't.

I was young, but I knew what they expected, as I followed Mel's directions to the home of Jill's non-griefed mother and twice-griefed father. I prayed, but my prayers bounced off the roof of my scratched, mint-green Plymouth, bounced back down into my throat and gathered there, gathered into a lump. Carl Sandburg said his poems always started with a lump in the throat. This lump wasn't the start of a poem.

What if I did say something that would get Jill's mother to accept the reality of her daughter's death? Would that make things any better? Her daughter was dead. There wasn't anything, ever, that would make that better. Why not just keep living with the hope that she would some day come home?

As always at the time of death, several friends and family members had gathered in the house behind a bulwark of cakes and casseroles and coffeepots. I met Jill's father. He asked me to talk to her mother. One of the women got her from a back room to come and meet the preacher. Wasn't it nice that he had just dropped by to say hello?

We sat in the kitchen, only the two of us. She was polite, distant. I asked about Jill. She explained that she would be home soon. I wondered out loud about that. She didn't seem to hear. I asked her if she knew why I had come. She didn't answer, just thanked me for coming, said it was nice to meet me, returned to her room. I went back to the living room. Her husband and I planned a funeral service for their daughter while she sat in a room down the hall in a private hell, a hell of suspension.

We had the funeral in the church building, even though Jill and her family weren't church people. It wasn't a large building. It seated a hundred and a half, maybe a few more counting the balcony, but you had to climb a let-down ladder to get up there; not many folks were brave enough for that. Still, it was twice as large as the funeral home, and the tragic death of a child or teen brings out twice as many people.

I wore my clerical collar. I'd just bought it a few weeks before. I was 25 and looked 20. All the hospitals I called in were Roman Catholic, before Vatican II, in the days of Latin masses and nursing nuns. A full white "pontiff" collar with a black shirt did wonders for getting a young Protestant pastor with a crew-cut around those hospitals. I had never before worn the backwards collar for anything but the hospitals. I didn't have to wear it in my own building to get around; everyone there knew who I was. I wore it now to remind me of who I was, what I represented, what I was called to do, to remind me that I was the way to the power, if anyone there could be such a way.

Marriage and potlucks and fatherhood and baseball have made my neck too big for the collar and my chest too broad for the shirt. I have other, larger, more discreet clerical shirts, in white and in muted liturgical colors, with precise little plastic tabs. We still have my first collar and shirt, though. My wife uses them for the skinny high-school-student preachers of the classroom weddings in her home economic classes.

I remember that I wore my plastic collar and my black shirt. That's all I remember . . . except for one other thing. As I stood up in the pulpit, as the last strains of the prelude waltzed down from the balcony out of our rollerink organ, Jill's mother slipped in the door.

She was dressed up—not quite enough for a funeral, but more than for shopping. She sat down on a metal folding chair, sideways, out of sight of everyone else, facing the door she had just squeezed through, her head turned toward me just enough that I could see her left eye.

Jesus said that the eye is the lamp of the body. It was to that lamp, April's lamp, and it alone, that I tried to carry the light, moving quickly over the heads of the people in the pews, reaching out to her before she could get out that door again. Jill's father and the rest of her family were in the front pew, but I was preaching to Jill's mother, about Jill, to her alone.

Why did Jill die so young? I don't know. *Did Jill or some-one else sin so grievously against God that the transcendent One is exacting punishment?* No. *Was it your fault, April?* No, you're suffering, but you're not being punished. *Is there more life for Jill?* Surely, although we have no idea what that is like. *Is God with us in this difficult time?* Yes. *Can we trust God, even though we don't understand?* Yes. *Does God really care about Jill and about us?* It's sometimes hard to believe, but yes, God cares. *Can you get through this?* Yes. Just barely, but yes.

I was preaching to Jill's mother, about Jill, but I was also preaching to me, about my own little daughter, trying to feel the grief as though it were Mary Beth, so that I might be able to understand just enough that something I might say could reach April, reach into the agonizing and lonely place of her anguish.

I couldn't think of anything else to say, so I stopped. Jill's mother slipped out the door.

I never saw her again. Each time I went to the house, her husband was polite, but he finally asked me to stop coming.

"She told me about the funeral, about how she came," he said. "You did what we asked you to do. You convinced her Jill was really dead. For April, well, you're the one who killed our daughter."

"i commend to your love and car© #..."

Preaching is dangerous because folks might actually believe what you say and act on it. I heard William Willimon tell the following story.

An older woman was in the hospital dying. Her pastor came to pray with her. She asked him to pray that she might be healed. He knew there was no chance of that; the doctors and nurses had told him so. She was too sick, too old, to get well. So he prayed that she might be made well, but that she'd have the grace to deal with what came, knowing that death would be what came. When he finished, she looked brighter. She sat up. She got out of bed. She began to walk. She went out in the hallway. She began to run. The last anyone saw of her, she was skipping down the street. The pastor walked out of the hospital, out to his car. He stood there, looking up to heaven in awe and amazement, and said, "Don't you *ever* do that to me again!"

Preachers get so used to an absence of response, or at least the absence of a visible response to our preaching, that we accept it. We make the best of it. We are the ones most surprised when a person responds.

When I was still in my 20s, one of my contemporaries told me of how he'd been invited to preach in a skid row mission. He took one of his best preaching class manuscripts with him. He said, "I was only about half-through when this drunk came up in front of the pulpit and yelled, 'I want to be saved.' He just kept yelling it. I had to get the ushers to come up and take him away so I could finish my sermon."

One of the things my general agent constantly told us, in my brief stint of selling life insurance after college, was: "If a person says, 'I want to buy,' don't say, 'I have to finish my sales presentation first.' Sell."

It's dangerous when people do respond, because we don't know how to handle it. It's also dangerous when they don't, because we begin to preach as though we expect nothing.

By response, I mean a life response to the Word, not just a verbal response to the words. Still, a preacher never knows what may happen in terms of immediate response, and you certainly remember those times when someone is so involved that she or he actually answers the preacher.

I was preaching about the men who made a hole in the roof of the house where Jesus was staying and lowered their paralytic friend down so Jesus could heal him. I asked what I thought was a rhetorical question: "What would we do if people were so anxious to hear the gospel that they made a hole in the roof to get in?" "We'd arrest 'em," yelled Lillie Foster. She was probably right.

I once listed the powers of darkness in the world. "Don't forget the Federal Reserve Board," real estate agent Vic Stenger called out.

Hazel Jones, Wayne Sherrow, May Everett, others who should remain nameless, a whole host of children . . . they had something to say, right then, in answer to my preaching. Those were days when the danger of boredom didn't reach us.

Probably the weakest part of any worship service is the opportunity for people to respond to whatever nudges from God they have felt. We try various symbolic things such as putting the offering last, claiming it is an offering of one's self rather than what we have left over in our purses at the end of the week. There's usually a hymn that has been carefully chosen by the preacher to sum up what she or he has tried to do in the service and sermon. The singers, and non-singers, notice mostly whether they like the tune, if it's one of "the old songs," which means one that was popular when they were children. Some of "the old songs" were written 20 years ago, whereas "the new ones" we don't know and don't like might be great hymns that have been sung for a thousand years.

For many generations in this country, an "altar call" was given at the end of the sermon, a summons from the preacher to get out of one's pew and walk to the communion railing, which we called the altar. There, kneeling, in prayer, one was to dedicate or rededicate oneself to God in response to the "message."

This was still the custom even when I started preaching, in rural areas at least, although it had begun to be controversial. It had not been a part of the regular worship services at Forsythe Church, although I had attended a revival service or two there where the evangelist gave highly emotional invitations that usually centered on getting someone to leave his cigarettes on the altar.

I hadn't the slightest idea what I would do if anyone came forward, but at the urging of the older members of my early congregations, I usually gave such a call. We then sang a hymn or two, waiting for some sinner to come forward, and when the person everyone was looking at stayed resolutely right where she or he had taken root, I gave a benediction, and we went home.

I was totally nonplussed the day a weeping, young, poor widow answered the call, prostrating herself over the railing. She was a regular at worship, well known to all of us. It was widely suspected that she was having an unlikely affair with an older, married man in the congregation who was kind to her and, having no children of his own, acted as a grandfather to her three. Various members made hand gestures to me, indicating I should go to her. They continued to sing. I knelt beside her. I was 20; she was 35. Haltingly, I prayed with her, not knowing what force had pulled her to the altar, not wanting to know.

I felt more comfortable giving invitations to church membership as a response rather than to conversion. When someone comes forward to join up, you know what's happening.

In one community where I preached there were several thousand bodies, but only one was black, a teenaged boy named *David. He was probably 80% white, but if you have a drop of black blood in you in this country, you're black. That was especially true in the 1960s. His mother was married to a white man, Polish by descent, so David was one of the few "black" people I ever knew with a surname that ended in "ski." David's parents didn't come to church, but he did. He also came to the youth group.

He was bright and handsome and athletic and polite. He was a good swimmer and worked as a lifeguard on the safety boat that patrolled the lake around which the town was scattered. It was alright for David to be on the boat and to save the lives of the white people who lived there and who came there as tourists. He did his lifesaving act with frequency, as the folks who went out on the lake were not noted for caution in the water, especially when they'd had a few beers. It was alright for him to be on the boat, but not alright for him to be on the shore. We could not have youth group meetings or picnics at the homes of church members whose property fronted on the lake, because no black person was allowed on the land around the lake. That included David.

When I went to be the pastor at that church, David had been attending worship and youth group there for several years, although he was not a member. I hadn't made any invitations to "respond" to the sermons in my first year there. I remembered too well that widow who had responded, and how I had no response for her.

At the end of my first year, at the annual conference, in front of all my colleagues and family, I was ordained a deacon, then the first of the two steps of ordination in the Methodist Church. Perhaps that official step emboldened me to think that there might be folks in our congregation who would answer God's call through my preaching.

A few Sundays later I made an invitation to respond to the Word of God, which I hoped I had preached in the sermon. I invited anyone who was not a member to come forward to join the church while we sang the closing hymn. On the last line of the hymn David slipped out of his row and marched resolutely down the center aisle, the steel heel taps of his black wingtips clacking above the sound of the organ on the green and cream tiles of the floor. He stood there by himself, at the center break of the altar rail, the only who had responded.

I went to him, stood before him, and started the ritual of membership, the questions to any new member. I read them from *The Book of Worship* presented to me by Bishop Richard Raines when he had ordained me recently.

"Do you here in the presence of God and this congregation renew the solemn promise and vow that was made at your baptism? Do you confess Jesus Christ as your Saviour and Lord and pledge your allegiance to his Kingdom? Do you receive and profess the Christian faith as contained in the New Testament of our Lord Jesus Christ? Will you be loyal to the Methodist church and uphold it by your attendance, your prayers, your gifts, and your service?"

David answered. "I do. I do. I do. I will."

One family, having themselves answered those same questions and taken those very vows not long before, got up and noisily stalked out, never to return. David heard them. Tears brimmed in his eyes, slipped over his lower lids, and ran down along his cheeks, but he did not look back. He reached out his hand for mine and held on tight as I continued: "David, the Lord defend thee with his heavenly grace and by his Spirit confirm thee in the faith and fellowship of all true disciples of Jesus Christ. Amen."

Then, "Brethren, I commend to your love and care David, whom we this day recognize as a member of the Church of Christ. What is your mind to him?"

They read from the hymnal: "We rejoice to recognize you as a member of the Church of Christ, and bid you welcome to all its privileges. Your peace, joy, and welfare are now our own. With you we renew our pledge to God and this church. The Lord bless you and keep you. The Lord make his face to shine upon you and be gracious unto you. The Lord lift up his countenance upon you and give you peace. Amen."

Then I read: "Brethren, I commend to your love and care David, whom we this day recognize as a member of the Church of Christ. Do all in your power to increase his faith, confirm his hope, and perfect him in love."

Preaching is dangerous. People might respond. David did. So did the family that walked out. So did the rest of the congregation, as they were required either to join those who left or to welcome this young black man into their midst as a brother within the love of God.

mayhem and marriage counseling

*Ray and *Opal had come to me several times for marriage counseling. Opal didn't know how to talk to Ray, so she didn't. Ray didn't know how to talk to Opal, so he "whacked her around" once in a while.

Opal had tried a few times to get the courage to tell him what she needed by getting drunk before he got home from work. The idea was that, fortified by liquid courage, when he arrived, she'd lay into him. She wasn't a drinker, though, and by the time he'd get home, she was so rubber-limbed and slubber-mouthed that Ray would end up rolling around on the floor laughing at her instead of hitting her. She was "better than television," he said.

That was the good part. The bad part was that they still didn't talk, didn't tell each other what they needed. I'd been working on that with them. Suddenly we started getting results. Not that they really talked to each other all that much, but Opal started acting happier, seemed much more content. Ray seemed to be happier, too. I was sure all those courses in pastoral counseling I was taking had made me into a whiz-bang marriage counselor. Maybe this was why I was called to ministry—to be a counselor, to help people with their problems, to apply what my professor Carrol Wise called "human help for human hurt."

Maybe, though, the change in Ray and Opal wasn't just my burgeoning skill as a counselor. There was also *Tom. Tom was Ray's best friend. They'd been in the army together. Tom lived only 30 minutes away, but they hadn't seen much of each other for several years. When Tom's wife left him, though, he started coming out to our blue collar suburb to spend time with Ray.

I was pleased. Ray needed more social life; he just went to work at a steel mill each day and then came home. He and

Opal depended on each other for their whole life outside of work, and neither of them was up to it. I'd gotten Ray to play on our church's team in the dart ball league,[1] but he treated that like work. I was sure that regular contact with a nice guy like Tom would be good for him. It seemed I was right. It wasn't just good for Ray, but for Opal, too. They had someone else around through whom they could talk to each other. They both began to blossom. They came to me less often.

Their place in my counseling was taken by Tom. He came to see me every once in a while to talk about his problems. He started coming to church.

His problems were contradictory: he was lonely, and he couldn't get away from his friends. He was lonely for real contact with real people. His friends were all in the area's organized crime mob, where he was a minor figure. Tom was tired of the life. He wanted out but didn't know how to get out. As we became friends, as his first step toward breaking with the mob, he gave me access to information I could feed to the Churchmen for Good Government, our group of ministers that was taking on the mob and its hold on the county government and policing.

After a few months Tom told me that just helping Churchmen for Good Government wasn't enough anymore. He had to get out.

"I've decided it's time for me to leave the life behind, get out of the mob, make a legit place for myself. I've found a good woman. I've never really had a good woman before, a woman I could love. I can't stay in the mob and expect her to love me."

"But won't they . . ."

"Nah, I don't think so. There's all that talk about how once you're in, they'll never let you out, but I'm not that high up. I just drive trucks, do odd jobs. They won't miss me."

I'd always wondered how Tom knew so much if he were as minor a figure in the mob as he claimed to be. Either he was a little higher than he acknowledged, or his friends decided they'd miss him more than he thought they would. Driving home one day on a six-lane highway, his car was crushed between two semi trucks and left in a ball of flame. The semis didn't stop.

Now here we were in a lower class funeral home in the city, staffed by a couple of guys who looked like they would never make any attempt to escape the mob. About 20 years later I saw those two guys again, when I went to a discount movie house to see "The Blues Brothers." In their narrow ties and dark suits and glasses, they were the early version of John Belushi and Dan Akroyd.

The purpose of a funeral is to help family and friends grieve well, not to grieve poorly. Overwhelming, screaming, body-wilting passion is not good grief. Passionate grief is like passionate anger; it doesn't "get it out of your system," but creates more of it in your system. Bad grief leads to more grief. Bad anger leads to more anger.

At first, Opal was doing good grief, just sniffling. Then an occasional muffled sob moaned through the wad of tissues she had balled in front of her face. Then her shoulders began to shake.

Not too bad so far. I didn't think she'd go much further. Tom was her husband's best friend, and he had spent a lot of time with them, but it wasn't like losing someone from your family.

Opal was a no-nonsense type of woman, not the sort to cry much over anything. She was working class, but had higher aspirations. She was secretary of the Womans Society of Christian Service (WSCS) at church, was thinking about branching out and joining other organizations, too. She was working on becoming higher class—a handkerchief dabber, not a tissue snorter. I had a lot of confidence in her ability to keep herself together. My confidence in her was misplaced.

By the time I'd done the opening Scripture and prayer, she was wailing. She almost drowned out the 23rd Psalm, and John 14 didn't have a chance. Ray hated scenes. He kept looking over his shoulder, silently imploring the other mourners to pay her no mind. When I started to preach, started defending God and blaming the mob for Tom's death, Ray got his arm around her and choked off enough of her oxygen that she could only hiccup. I was appreciative but tried to keep from showing it.

When I finished and it was time for us to get in our cars for the long ride to the cemetery, Ray got Opal on her feet and hustled her off to the basement where the restrooms were. I waited upstairs, seeing others into their cars, waiting for Ray and Opal to reappear, hoping Opal had gotten under control with a good nose-blowing in the ladies room. It was a long wait, but we couldn't have gone to the cemetery without them even if we'd wanted to; their car was second in line behind the hearse.

They finally came back up the stairs, as they had gone, Ray dragging Opal by an arm. She acted like she wasn't seeing too well, and the reason was obvious. The right side of her face was red and welted, and her right eye was already swelling shut.

The idiot's gone and done it again, I thought to myself, can't handle his grief, so he's taking it out on her . . .

I started toward them. I figured I could take Ray. He had street smarts, outweighed me by 50 pounds, and was steel-mill strong, but I was 15 years his junior and had a longer reach. I'd never been in a fist fight in my life, but I wasn't about to tolerate something like this as part of a funeral service. Behind his back, though, Opal waved me off. I stopped to think about it, and that cost me my chance. They were past me and out the door and into the car before I could decide what to do.

I got into the front seat of the hearse with the younger of the funeral directing Blues Brothers. We rode in silence to the cemetery. When we got there, Opal staggered getting out of the car. Her other eye was beginning to close up.

The graveside committal is never long, but that one was probably the shortest I ever did. Ray started to drag Opal away again, but I was quicker this time and got between them and their car. Other mourners began drifting away, looking back over their shoulders at us.

"What the ____'s going on?" I hissed.

"Didn't you wonder why she was all broke up, the whore? He was my best friend, sure, but that's not worth blowing a hole in your pants over. Turns out he was her best friend, too, the whore. . . ."

Then it all came clear. . . . Tom telling me he'd found a good woman, Opal so content lately, no longer worried about her communication with Ray, more stricken at the funeral than any of Tom's own family . . .

". . . didn't even deny it. Took her down to the basement, and she blurts it out, the whore, how she's been doing it with him every time she got the chance . . ."

"Ray, I'm awfully sorry. You've got grief piled on grief. You ought to be able to mourn Tom, and now you can't. But you can't hit Opal anymore. We're just going to have to let this ride for a little bit and then sort it out. I think I'd better take Opal . . ."

She waved me off again. Tears were almost squirting out through her closing eyelids. I didn't know whether it was the pain in her face or the pain in her heart that was pushing them like that.

"I want to be with Ray," she whispered.

Ray tilted his head over to the side, avoiding my gaze. A tear began to run down his cheek, too. It was small and reluctant, but it was a tear.

"It's okay, Rev. I won't hit her anymore. God, I don't want to hit her . . ."

I followed them in my VW beetle, the old type, with the natural flow heater, trying to get up enough speed that a little of the warm air would be forced in on my cold feet and numb heart, praying, thinking, mourning, praying some more, wondering a little how'd we explain to the WSCS why their secretary couldn't see to read the minutes at their meeting the next day.

I parked in their driveway behind them and followed them into the three-bedroom ranch on a slab, even though they didn't invite me. Ray slumped into a chair at the kitchen table. Opal fumbled around, making coffee mostly by feel. I went over to help her, but she waved me away again. I sat down in the chair I knew Tom always used.

"We'd probably better talk about this."

"No," said Ray. "Not me," said Opal.

"You ever going to talk to me again about your problems?"

"Not me," said Ray. "No," said Opal.

"You going to talk to each other?"

"Yes," said Opal. Ray nodded.

"You going to tell me what you say?"

"No," said Ray. Opal started to shake her head, then winced.

"Good," I said.

Opal set a cup of coffee in front of Ray, slumped down in a side chair with one for herself. I started out the back door.

"Say goodbye to Tom for me, will you?"

"Okay," said Ray. Opal nodded, slowly.

Ray became our heaviest triples hitter in the dart ball league. Opal had moved up to vice-president of the WSCS by the time the bishop sent me to my next appointment.

note

[1] A square dart board, about 4' wide and 5' high, contains a baseball field. Sections are marked for strikes, balls, outs, hits of all sorts, etc. Regular baseball rules are used. Darts are thrown underhand. It was a very popular winter activity for church and social leagues in Northwest Indiana in the early 1960s. I have no idea if it is still played anywhere.

prote⑤tants behind bars

St. Augustine said, "There is larceny in the heart." The bank robbers must have seen into my heart, for they chose me.

Prisoners in those days didn't organize themselves so much by race as by crime. I didn't know that. All I knew was that Norm Kherli, the chaplain at the federal penitentiary at Terre Haute, Indiana, had invited me, along with several other area ministers, to spend a Lenten retreat day with the Protestant Brotherhood. After we had worshiped together in the bare prison chapel, each minister helping to lead the worship, the brotherhood members divided themselves up into discussion groups for the rest of the day.

"We want him," said the bank robbers, pointing at me. I didn't know if it was an honor or a curse.

It turned out that they wanted me because, as a new seminary graduate and a campus minister at Indiana State University and Rose Polytechnic Institute, they thought I would be an intellectual. After all, I associated daily with all those Ph.Ds.[1] The bank robbers and the one counterfeiter they allowed into the group were very intellectual.

I didn't feel especially intellectual that day. It was my first time in prison, my first time in a jail of any kind, if you don't count high school biology class. Through the years I've had church members who felt I should spend more time in prison, but just walking in that day was enough to make me want to walk right back out again. But I couldn't. Those steel doors, rank upon rank, had clanged shut behind me. I began to understand a little bit, inside those gray walls, of why they call it "stony lonesome."

I did most of the talking that day. When I became embarrassed and tried to involve others in the discussion, they said: "Hey, we spend a lot of time together. We've heard everything any of us has ever thought, over and over again.

We want to hear new ideas." I listened enough, however, to do some learning about prison life.

I learned that they called the process of entering prison, of getting a number in place of a name, "debaptizing." In traditional Christian faith, at baptism you get what we call your "Christian" name, your first name, to be added to your "family" name. The minister even asks the parents, "What name shall be given this child?"—even though it's already been given, and we all know what it is. In churches that practice adult baptism there is usually a christening service for infants when that same naming takes place. When you enter your prison, your name is taken away. You are debaptized. You must, within those walls, decide again what name you want to bear. "Christian" is a hard name to carry in prison.

"Without the support of one another in this fellowship," the bank robbers said, "none of us would ever make it. You can't be a Christian by yourself in prison."

You can't be a Christian *anywhere* by yourself, I reminded them. But in prison the requirement of rebaptism, of choosing your identifying name daily, is so much more obvious than it is on what they call the "outside."

I learned of the informal sociological and psychological research they had been doing, of the bank robber profile they had developed. They had simply listed all their individual characteristics and compared them. The characteristics they all had were what made a bank robber. First on the list was that, growing up, they all had bad or nonexistent relationships with their fathers. So had I. Maybe that's why they had chosen me.

They told me of their disdain for Karl Barth's book, *Deliverance to the Captives,* a collection of sermons the great theologian had preached in prison in Switzerland. They felt Barth understood nothing of prison life. Being a classic southern Indiana backwoods liberal hillbilly, I thought he understood nothing of theology. I was sounding more like a bank robber all the time.

I met *Herb. While he was out of the room, for what I learned was a regular meeting with the warden, the other bank robbers told me his story.

He had been a Baptist preacher in Memphis. Times were hard. His congregation was poor. His children were sick. He was too proud to ask for help. He robbed a bank.

As soon as he had done it, he realized that he'd slipped a cog. He went to some men in his church and told them what he had done. They went with him to the police. He returned all the money. He hadn't used a weapon, and no one was hurt. It was a first offense. The judge gave him 40 years.

He'd been in 10 years when I first met him. The prison warden had been trying to get him a new trial, or a pardon, or a sentence reduction, for all those 10 years. He was a model prisoner. He was as much a chaplain to the other prisoners as anyone on the staff. He was 42 years old. His wife had divorced him. He never heard from his children. He was unfailingly kind. He never smiled.

I asked what I could do. There wasn't much. The judge who'd sentenced him had died. Most of the witnesses were dead or lost. No one in the judicial system wanted to open a dead case.

The whole time we lived in Terre Haute, I kept going out to the prison, meeting with the bank robbers until they knew as much about my ideas as they did about one another's. Each time I left them, each time I went back outside, I felt vaguely guilty.

It was at the annual banquet my last year that I met Brother Hood himself. His name was Hood, so in the Protestant Brotherhood, he just had to be Brother Hood. He was black. I wasn't used to black prisoners. There were many in the brotherhood, but all the bank robbers were white.

Brother Hood had been outside, operating construction equipment and working as an assistant pastor at a church.

He'd been invited back to speak at the annual banquet. We ate the regular prison food, but we were in a room by ourselves. Brother Hood gave a supremely eloquent sermon.

"When I comed here, ta this pen, I cudn' read or write. I joined this here bro'hood, 'n you done taughtn me how ta read 'n write. You hept me git my high school diploma so I cud git my 'quipment certificate and git a job on the outside. You done taughtn me ta read the Scriptures. You done taughtn me 'bout Jesus. Because I bin here, in this bro'hood, I is a part of you, an' you is a part of me. If I don' make it on the outside, you don' make it either. If I make it, you dun made it, too."

I was sitting across the table from Herb. He smiled.

note

[1]Neither they nor I knew then that some Ph.D.s can be the least intellectual people you'll ever talk to.

"Don't look at them," she whispers. "Don't make eye contact. Look straight ahead. We're going to hear Dr. King. Just think about that."

It is the voice of the Negro student, marching between me and the line of National Guardsmen with the Confederate flag patches on their shoulders. She is experienced.

"They're more likely to take a swipe at a white man," she had said when we first arrived, "especially one from the North. I'll stay between you and them. They don't want some photographer getting a picture of them beating up on a darkie girl."

"How would they know I'm from the North?"

"You're a white man, and you're marching to Montgomery [Alabama] to hear Dr. King. That's how they'll know."

The National Guard has been called out to protect the marchers from the Klan and the rest of the population of Alabama, even though the general feeling is that they are more likely to be our attackers than our protectors. She is our first line of defense against our defenders, this brave young black Methodist college student from Alabama.

She is why we are here in the first place. The Alabama Methodist Student Movement called us up in Indiana and said, "Come down and march with us. We're going to walk the last day of the march from Selma to Montgomery. We're going to rally in front of the capital to listen to Martin Luther King. We want you to march with us."

It reminded me very much of the apostle Paul's Macedonian call: "Come over and help us."

I look around at the folks to my left. I've positioned myself just inside our student guide. I think of myself as the second line of defense, after her. They'll have to come through me to get to André Hammonds or Bob Mullins. I'm especially worried about André. He is black, a professor of sociology at Indiana State University, a specialist in the sociology of religion. Folks down here don't like "uppity niggers" with Ph.D.s from the University of Tennessee. Bob is white, a journalism major from Hammond, Indiana, the student president of our Wesley Foundation. We are the representatives from Terre Haute—a campus minister, a professor, and a student.

There are others, from other Indiana campuses—Indiana University, Ball State, Evansville College (now the University of Evansville), Purdue. More campus ministers and professors and students, mostly white. We gathered in Bloomington, early in the morning, to climb aboard our chartered DC-3.

They all got to see me throw up on my first plane ride. The air was considerably turbulent, but I was more than considerably nervous. My first plane ride and my first civil rights march—together! When I answered the call to ministry, it never occurred to me that it was a telephone call from Alabama.

As we fly, the stewardess moves up and down the aisle, chatting politely, but distantly. She suggests that we are "outside agitators." We explain that we were invited to come by Alabama people. She seems unimpressed.

The co-pilot comes back and chats with us, politely but distantly. He suggests that we need to give people time to change. We explain that it's been a hundred years since the Civil War and that there's been no progress on race relations since then, more time than anyone in the U.S. has been alive. He seems unimpressed.

The pilot comes back and chats with us, politely but distantly. He suggests that we should be working through the courts and the legislatures to make change instead of "marching in the streets" and "breaking the laws." We explain that it's the courts and the legislatures, and the laws they have made and enforce, that create the problem. We explain that we must answer to the higher law of God. He seems unimpressed.

Helen has packed a huge sack of sandwiches and carrot sticks for me. When the plane starts lurching and I start regurging, I don't even want to admit that the lunch exists. André passes it around the plane, and everyone else eats my lunch. Now I'm weak and hungry and thirsty and light-headed, walking this last leg of the march from Selma to Montgomery.

I think about my wife and two little daughters, wonder what I'm doing in Alabama, leaving them back home in Indiana, worrying about me. I don't know it, but Phyllis Graham has canceled her math classes at Indiana State University and come down Ninth Street to spend the day with Helen and the girls. Phyllis and I were classmates at Oakland City High School. Now she's sitting with my wife, playing with my daughters, filling up the empty space of worry, doing what friends do. Later, I will be one of the pastors at her wedding. We are still friends.

I'm weak not only from hunger, but also from worry. There's strength in numbers, and there are thousands of us here. Most of the beatings and murders of freedom riders and civil rights workers are committed in the dark, or at least away from the eye of the reporters and the television cameras.

Not always, though. We've seen pictures on television and in the newspapers, the police with their riot batons and water hoses and big dogs, the rednecks with their ax handles and heavy boots. When the children of violence lash out, when they get that first taste of power, there is no restraining them. They seem not to care that the whole world, or even God, is watching.

I know that God is watching, to see if I will be faithful to the call.

We finally stop walking. We stand in the sun and watch and listen as Martin Luther King, Jr., the young Baptist pastor, the young Ph.D. from Boston University, stands in front of the Alabama capital, under the Confederate flag, and tells us why we are there. He says it is because God is watching, to see if we will be faithful to the call. I know that God is speaking through this Martin Luther, nailing his theses on the door of the Alabama Statehouse. I know that I am called, not only to preach the good news of deliverance with my mouth, but also with my feet, standing on Alabama blacktop, and even with my churning stomach.

After the march we are bused back to the Montgomery airport. Our pilot keeps asking for permission to take off. There is giggling from the tower, and we are told to wait.

"These idiots," says the pilot. "The weather's getting worse by the second. There's a hurricane coming in off the coast."

More giggling from the tower. Finally, we are put into the air. The hurricane winds are chasing us. The pilot is pushing the plane to the limit.

"They put us up in this on purpose, those _____ fools," he curses. "We'll never make it. They think it's funny. We've got to get out of this."

He lands the plane in Birmingham. The pilot and the co-pilot send the stewardess off to a hotel, but they refuse to leave the plane. It will be morning before we can get into the air again.

We try to buy food at the airport restaurant. They refuse to serve us. We send in, by herself, a little white-haired, white-skinned education professor. She's a grandmother and looks the part. She has a southern accent. She asks sweetly for a couple of sandwiches. They know who she is. She comes back empty-handed.

One of us knows the Unitarian pastor in Birmingham. He telephones him. Before long, several Unitarian Fords and Chevies come to get us. They take us to their church building, a lovely stone and brick edifice on a large rose-bushed lot in one of the nicest parts of town. Their people bring in food from their own kitchens and feed us. I can eat now. Southern Unitarian food tastes very much like southern Baptist or Methodist food.

I notice shadows passing by the windows and suspect the "inside agitators," the children of violence, have caught up with us.

"Not to worry," the Unitarians say. "They *have* bombed us a couple of times, but they didn't do much damage. Now we patrol outside the building every night. Those are only Unitarian shadows you see."

A lot of folks, especially in Alabama, think Unitarians aren't really Christian. Right now, I'm glad those shadows don't belong to the local "Christians."

The Unitarians divide us up. André and Bob and I, along with five other men, are driven to the home of a Unitarian physician. We can't see the neighborhood very well in the dark, but it looks like Doggyville, not Dog Patch. The house is large. We're two to a room without displacing any family members and without sharing beds, and only four of us to a bathroom.

We eat breakfast in a sunny dining room.

"Stay away from the windows," the teenaged daughter tells us.

I look around. The houses are bigger than the fraternities back at Indiana State. They sit on huge, landscaped, manicured lawns. This is the nicest neighborhood in which I've ever spent a night. It's not the kind of neighborhood where you have to stay away from the windows.

"Was there any garbage on the lawn?" the mother asks the daughter.

"No. Yesterday was pick-up day. Must not have had any left."

The doctor's wife explains: "We're Alabamans. We've lived here a long time. We've always gotten along fine with our neighbors; no reason not to. Then this civil rights business came up. Naturally, we said Negroes ought to have the same rights as anybody else. Our neighbors didn't agree. When we started having Negro folks into our house as guests instead of as servants, they started dumping their garbage on our lawn."

"I'm a junior in high school," the daughter tells us. "Before, I was getting straight A's. Always have. Now I'm getting straight F's. I'm dropping out. Vasser's going to let me come early and just go ahead and start college."

She looks out the window at the magnolias.

"It's okay. I'm ready to go. I was sort of looking forward to the prom, though," she says.

Breakfast is over. The Unitarian cars come to get us. We thank our hostess and start to walk out the front door.

"Wait," she urges, peering out a small pane of glass beside the door. "Let's wait and see whether they drive up to the door."

I sneak a peek from the corner of a window. I see ruts in the soft green sod of the front yard. Sure enough, the first car drives right across the yard, straight up to the front door.

"He must have seen something, so he doesn't want to wait out in the drive for you to walk down the stones. When you go out the door, do it on the fly, and get right into the car. Keep your heads down. Sometimes our neighbors shoot at our guests out of their upstairs windows."

The driver, a local professor, has the Ford's back door already open. Bob and I flank Andre, and we dive in. We back up to the drive so the other car can wallow through the sod, up to the front door, to pick up the others.

We drive by palatial estates. You've got to have big money to live here, I think. I remember what the Howell House children said about Evanston: "Only a gangster would have enough money to live in a house like this." These are the homes of executives and lawyers and factory owners and bankers. They're the people who throw garbage on the lawns of their neighbors, who shoot at their neighbors' guests out of their upstairs windows. We'd be safer in the "bad" section of the city. It is a strange thought.

Our pilot and co-pilot have slept in the plane, in their clothes. The stewardess has stayed in a hotel, but she doesn't look like it was a happy experience. They take turns chatting with us on the way home, passionately, closely.

"My God, we had no idea what this was like. We don't even like you people. We didn't even want to bring you down here. They tried to kill us just because we were with you. Something's got to be done about this."

Something is being done, I think, not by people like you or me, but by people who live here. By people who have the courage of their convictions. By Baptist folks who say, "I'll walk before I'll ride in the back of the bus." By Unitarian folks who say, "I'll miss my prom and pick up the garbage off the yard before I'll make someone else ride in the back of the bus." Although for me it's only for a day, I'm proud to be on the journey with these local Joshuas, marching around the city until the back of the bus falls off.

In the spring of 1995 Helen and I visit our younger daughter, Kathleen, and her husband, Patrick. They're teaching at Auburn University. We drive over to Selma, stand at the Edmund Pettus Bridge, retrace my Montgomery route of 30 years before. In Selma, we see white children and black children, all in green and tan uniforms, coming out of school together at the end of the day.

My daughter's neighborhood in Auburn is modest. Her next-door neighbors are black. Nobody throws garbage on the lawn. Nobody shoots at us when we get in the car.

"first, do no harm."

That's the opening line of the physician's oath. Preachers are physicians, too, physicians of the soul. So the very first time a preacher mounts to the pulpit, and every time thereafter, when she or he raises an arm for the first gesture, it should be as a token of the same vow: "First, do no harm."

There is immense potential for doing harm from the pulpit. Every word from a preacher's mouth is uttered through a megaphone of authority that is two thousand years old. There are many good thinkers in those pews who will not be wounded by truthless shots from the pulpit. Those folk will sift the wheat from the chaff for themselves. There are others, however, who will believe every word, just because the preacher, the one called by God and ordained by the church, said it. If that word is hopeless or faithless or simply wrong, we have put that person in harm's way.

Wesley Foundations didn't have Sunday worship of their own when I went to college and started in campus ministry. Students were expected to attend the Methodist Church nearby, usually located right next door, and the Wesley Foundation minister was "attached" to that church, in some indefinable way, for purposes of worship leadership. So it was in Terre Haute, Indiana. I was usually allowed to read the Scripture or give the pastoral prayer. Only once a semester was I allowed to preach, so I always had a lot of thought and passion stored up. It was under those circumstances that Phyllis Graham first heard me preach.

Phyllis was a professor of mathematics at Indiana State University, a new Ph.D. from Indiana University, and a pool shark without peer. We had gone to high school together. Her father was the pastor at Oak Grove General Baptist Church, a mile down the road from Forsythe Church. Those two free-standing and free-thinking country churches did Christmas programs and vacation Bible schools together.

Phyllis had known me before my strange calling, before I had any reason to speak with any authority. Now she came to Centenary Church to hear me preach all that stored-up thought and passion.

She waited until everyone else had left, then slipped up to me and grabbed a fistful of robe and pulled me down to her face.

"You may not know it yet," she whispered fiercely, "but you're something special in that pulpit. When you get up there, people believe what you say. You be _____ careful what it is."

riots and rumors
of riots

My wife was a whiter shade of pale. "They said I'd better not come down here, because bad things are going to happen. I'm scared." This from a woman who's terrified of spiders but had never before been frightened by middle-aged men in funny little blue and yellow hats.

It had all started routinely enough. The student cabinet of our Wesley Foundation at Illinois State University had planned a series of Sunday evening supper discussions about the war in Vietnam. It's the sort of thing campus religious groups did in the '50s and '60s. Some still do. We always had a Sunday evening discussion series going on one topic or another. The dormitory cafeterias didn't serve a Sunday supper, so we could usually lure a large group of students for any program with the promise of cheap food. Helen and I had met as undergraduates one autumn evening, at the Wesley Foundation at Indiana University, folding the crimson-on-cream program cards that detailed the Sunday evening programs for that year. Naturally, I always had a special fondness for Sunday evening programs.

Our Vietnam series started with a history professor who gave us the historical background of the Vietnam conflict. Bad pudding. Nice presentation. Interesting discussion.

The next week we had a geography lecture on Southeast Asia, complete with slides. Bad tuna casserole. Nice photography. Interesting discussion.

Then this week. Our student programming committee had invited two young men from the Chicago Area Draft Resistance Effort (CADRE) to speak about why they were opposed to the war. This was early in the war resistance period. Almost everyone on our campus still unquestioningly supported American military involvement in Vietnam.

Our students had invited the CADRE boys because they didn't agree with them. They wanted to let them know that. Bad chili. An invasion by the local American Legion. Interesting discussion.

We'd heard rumors, and there had been some ominous phone calls. One threatened our daughters, ages four and six. Another threatened to blow up our house. More calls had come to the office of the local church. The minister of the church decided not to say anything about them to us. Later he told me he hadn't passed the information along to me because he suspected the callers were members of the church. He "didn't want to get involved in a squabble between the church and Wesley Foundation." We thought of threats against us and our children as being quite a bit more than a squabble between two church organizations.

We began to drive our first grade daughter to school instead of letting her walk, but we weren't sure the threats and the Vietnam series were connected. This CADRE thing was just another Sunday evening discussion. Why would anyone get upset about that?

Upset they were, though, the middle-aged men in the blue and yellow "overseas" caps. Some of them had fueled their upsetness with an afternoon of imbibing at the local hall. Some of them were in uniforms and parts of uniforms. And some of them had threatened my wife with vague suggestions of violence as she entered the doors of the church and started down the stairs to the campus ministry area of the building we shared with the local congregation.

"They've just sort of taken over the entryway," she whispered. "They're literally blocking the stairs and telling the students that bad things will happen to them if they come down here. I don't know how many they've scared away already."

"How did you get down here?" I asked.

"There was a big shave-headed galoot in a brown uniform standing right in front of the stairs. He seemed to be the ring leader. I just shoved him out of the way and came on down," she said.

Not many students had the chutzpah to do that. We already had a fairly full house, though. Most of those who attended the program usually came for supper an hour earlier. There were always a dozen or two who slipped in just in time for the program itself, though. I had wondered why they hadn't shown up yet. Down in the basement we hadn't realized that upstairs we'd been invaded and unwanted "ushers" were turning people away.

Fortunately, the young men from CADRE hadn't arrived yet. That gave me a little time to operate. I called several of the prettiest girls together.

"If any strange men come down the stairs, welcome them, put name tags on them, and offer them seats, just like we do anyone else."

Then I got the boys together.

"If any strange men come down the stairs, let the girls handle them."

Sure, it was sexist, although we didn't know that word then. I was counting on the sexism of the Legionnaires and their fellow-travelers to make it work in our favor. I'd do it again.

I went up the back stairway, slipped into the church office, and telephoned the police chief, Bill Bray. He and I belonged to the local Lion's Club. We almost always sat together for Tuesday lunch. The "lion tamer" had to think twice about "tail twisting" at the table of the chief and the preacher.

"Bill, I hate to bother you at home on a Sunday evening, but there's a bunch of guys blocking our doors and turning people away. I'm afraid things are going to get ugly. Any chance you could come down here?"

He got a few more facts from me, then said . . .

"Just stall. Don't start any program stuff until I get there."

That sounded fine to me. I slipped back down the stairs, made sure the girls were positioned near the doors, and let the after-supper conversations continue.

In about 15 minutes the doors burst open, and a whole motley herd of old and middle-aged white men burst in, led by the surly-looking, skin-headed galoot in the brown uniform. They were immediately besieged by pretty young girls welcoming them and asking them to fill out name tags and to come over to the program area and have seats. Confused by all the attention, some actually filled out name tags; others let themselves be led to folding chairs. Most tried to act macho, but the effect was destroyed because they glanced over their shoulders a lot, like someone was gaining on them.

Somebody was. The reason for the backward glances strode through the door. Here was the chief, herding the stragglers into the room, simply by the force of his presence. Several inches above my 6'1" and 100 pounds beyond my 180, Bill could fill up a room quite easily by himself. He had muscles on his muscles. His head was shaved, too, but the absence of hair didn't reveal just skin. Even his scalp, even his ears, had muscles.

He was big as we sat together for Tuesday lunches, but on this Sunday night he was bigger than he'd ever been before. It was "The Uniform."

To the best of my knowledge, no one in our town had seen him in The Uniform before. He had been in town only a year. He was a low-key, plain-clothes kind of guy. Now he was dressed in an enormous, barrel-shaped, double-breasted blue suit. Dark blue stripe down the side of the pants. Gold piping on the cuffs and pockets. Chief's insignia on the lapels. Brass buttons. Gold epaulettes. Medals. All this topped by a flat, billed officer's hat. Gold piping and buttons on it, too. The lines of the uniform were clean, no weapons of any kind. It was a clear statement: "I don't need any weapons."

"You came to hear the program," I heard him saying to the stragglers, "and you'll hear the program."

They hadn't come to hear the program, of course. They had come to disrupt it, but who was going to tell him that? Sulkily, they dragged in, glared at the girls who welcomed them, and finally found seats.

Caught up in the chief's sweep were some trustees of the church. I was surprised to see them. Among the church members, only a few professors ever came to Wesley Foundation programs, but they were of that rank who think students are important. Thus, they were neither trusted nor taken seriously by the administration, of either the university or of the church. When I tried to welcome the trustees, it quickly became clear that they had come to lend their gray-suited and striped-tie support to the forces of olive drab and yellow and gold.

The trustees refused to sit in the chairs in the program area, apparently thinking that would imply cooperation of some sort. Instead, they sat on tables in the back, under the sign that asked all and sundry not to sit on the tables. These were bankers and store owners and industry managers, men in their 40s and 50s, vice-presidents, the sort who like to enforce rules such as not sitting on tables. I pointed the sign out to them and asked them to come up to the chairs. They refused to move. The tables broke under their considerable weight about midway through the program. They sat on the kitchen counter for the rest of it. Later I sent them a bill to replace the table. They never replied.

Behind the chief were a few students who just happened to come at the right time to gain admission while the chief was forcing everyone down the stairs. Finally, straggling in at the rear, came a couple of long-haired, bell-bottomed "peaceniks"—the boys from CADRE—who hadn't been able to find the place and thus fortunately had not arrived before the chief was there.

I later learned that Bill had several cars of his officers, equipped with riot gear, outside the church building. They could be on the scene in 10 seconds if he needed them. He had parked them around the corner, though, so that no one would know they were there. Unlike police officers who trust in a show of force, he knew that the very presence of the police can provoke trouble. Also, I think he had a great trust in the power of one man—properly dressed, without weapons.

The chief waited until everyone was seated. Then he stepped to the front of the room, beside the piano. He drew himself up to his full height, which by this time seemed very full, indeed. He stood at attention, his hat tucked under his arm.

"I want everyone to know," he said, "that I am a twice-wounded veteran of the Korean war. My presence here does not imply agreement or disagreement with anything that might be said here. But the law says that nobody can break up anybody else's meeting, and in this town, I *am* the law. That means if anybody here wants to break up this meeting, they'll have to break me up first. Is that clear?"

He waited. You could have heard the tiniest fragment of a pin drop. He spoke again, a little softer.

"Is that clear?"

The silence got as thick as the chocolate pudding we'd just had for supper. The chief seemed satisfied. He turned to me and nodded. I nodded to the student chairman of the program committee. He stood, cleared his throat, and introduced the young men from CADRE.

They sat at ease in front of the group, explaining in a quiet and logical way why they refused to fight in Vietnam. The chairman asked for questions. The boys of wars past shouted out "questions" such as "You're just cowards," and "Why don't you go back to Russia where you belong?" and "You're traitors to the flag," and "You're getting our boys killed because you're not supporting the war."

The CADRE boys took each shout seriously, explaining that they really weren't cowards, but that they thought this war was wrong, that they hadn't come from Russia and weren't Communists, that they respected the flag and would fight for their country under other circumstances, that they thought the best way to support our boys and keep them from getting killed was to get them out of Vietnam. Of course, they never got to answer a comment fully before another handful of insults was flung at them.

There were two young men among the older Legionnaires. They were flesh-gaunt and crew-cut and t-shirted. After awhile one of them raised a hand and said he had a question.

"Yeah," came a chorus from the older men. "Listen to these boys. They've been there. They know what it's about. They're not afraid."

The men in the blue and yellow caps relaxed down into their folding chairs, arms crossed, satisfied that now the young war protesters would be put in their place by men of equal youth but greater experience and courage.

But the young man stood and said: "It's true that I've been there, to Vietnam. I understand why anyone wouldn't want to go."

The older men began to stir uneasily. The young man beside him nodded his head.

"It's hell there," he went on. "Nobody should want to go to hell. I've seen things I never want to see again. I've done things I never want to do again. But it is our country's war."

He spoke very directly now to the young men from CADRE, oblivious to the other persons in the room, wanting sense from what he had experienced, not caring where the answers came from, as long as they were true.

"We really do have to stand up against people who are doing bad things, don't we? If you don't want to fight, I understand that. I don't want to fight anymore, either. But you could go as medics, couldn't you? You would be helping people; you wouldn't be killing."

Gradually the rest of us in the room were becoming spectators. The other young man in the t-shirt had stood up beside his friend. The young men in the bell-bottoms had stood, too. The rest of us continued to sit. This discussion was now literally above our heads. This was a meeting of the young lions, the young men of war, those who fought it and those who opposed it. It was clear that the crew-cuts in the t-shirts and the long-hairs in the bell-bottoms knew there were questions they could only answer together, questions that old men and onlookers could not understand, still less answer, the questions of young men, the questions of honor and courage and conscience.

The boys from CADRE explained that they had considered being medics, but to do so would still be support of a war they felt was wrong.

"What about being conscientious objectors, then? You'd do alternate service, maybe even go to jail, but it would be an honorable thing to do."

"Yes, we've thought of that, too, but it would still be playing by the rules of the system, and it's the system that makes us fight this immoral war. We have to stand up against the system."

"Would you go to Canada before you'd go to jail?"

"No. Going to Canada isn't protest; it's just escape. We'd rather go to jail. At least people would know we have the courage of our convictions."

"We understand why you won't fight. We don't agree with you, but you are honorable men, and we respect that."

"And we understand why you do fight. We think you are wrong, and we wish you would join us as protesters, but we respect your position, too. You are honorable men."

Their discussion took much longer, of course. I've just summarized it here. It sounds almost quaint today, to hear young men speaking of honor, to hear them agree to disagree about something so passionate and divisive, to remember that they actually said to one another, "You are honorable men."

The hour of closure had come. I thanked the boys from CADRE and everyone else for coming. I invited the locals to come back the next Sunday night when we would serve macaroni and cheese and have a program on whether the student government should take a stand on the war.

The meeting broke up quietly. Folks milled around for a bit, trying to figure out what had happened, not sure if it was time to go. One of the brave supper eaters was Don Ruthenberg, the chairman of our Wesley Foundation board, the dean of students at Illinois Wesleyan University, just a mile down the street. He approached the big skinhead in the brown uniform, the man I had started to think of as a cartoon character. In my mind I was calling him "uniform man."

"Why are you wearing a uniform?" asked the dean.

"I'm in the reserves," uniform man answered, a bit disdainfully. "I was on maneuvers this weekend."

"How long have you been off maneuvers?" asked the dean, for he knew that a reservist wasn't permitted to wear his uniform just any time he wanted to, like to invade a church. When reserve duty was over, he had to be out of that uniform within a specified few hours.

"What do you know about it?" uniform man sneered, making it fairly clear that he had exceeded his time limit.

Don wouldn't back off. "How come you've got a knife in your boot?" he asked.

"You don't know anything, do you? Paratroopers always carry knives in their boots."

"That's strange," said the dean. "I jumped 22 times in World War II, and I never had a knife in my boot."

Uniform man was getting a little desperate now. "Well then, you weren't an officer. . . ."

"I was a captain. Captains were officers in World War II. Are captains not officers in the reserve?"

He said it mildly, but uniform man was backing up, toward the door. The dean kept advancing, staying toe to toe with him. Without a word, uniform man turned around and scurried up the stairs and out of the building.

Don turned to me and smiled. "Do you think I should have mentioned that I jumped as a chaplain?" he asked.

Although no reporters were present, that night a local radio station reported that the students of the Wesley Foundation had rioted while demonstrating against the war and that it took several carloads of police in riot gear to quell the disturbance. The local newspaper quoted the radio report the next day. I called both station and newspaper. The station wouldn't talk to me. The newspaper, citing "confidential sources," which I assumed to be either the trustees or the Legionnaires, would neither retract its story nor print a "letter to the editor" I submitted. I learned that when a newspaper says "We stand by our story," it doesn't necessarily mean they think the story is true. It just means they stand by their story.

I returned 26 years later to the scene for a special occasion. It was the retirement celebration for Anne Paxton, the Wesley Foundation office secretary I had hired the year of the invasion. She had mentioned to a church lady that I was going to be there for her party.

"Oh, I remember him," the church lady said. "He was the campus minister here when the Wesley Foundation students rioted and the police had to come."

looking good

I was in my early 30s when I began to go bald. I no more anticipated baldness than I had a call to ministry nor than I would cancer. None of these were in my genes.

Ministry was only on the edges of my family history. Before me, there had been one minister in the entire extended family, my father's Uncle Elmer Smith, brother of my grandmother. He left farming and became an Evangelical United Brethren pastor when he was 40. He had a family who needed a place to live and something to eat, so he was appointed to serve a church, and presumably receive a salary, in Piqua, Ohio, while he went to college and seminary.

Delighted with the whole college experience after 25 years of farming, he decided to go out for the football team. The first game he ever saw, he lined up at right guard, long before helmets and pads and shoes amounted to an industry. His congregation wasn't quite sure what to think when he hobbled into the pulpit the next morning, wearing the colors of black and blue, the day after his first game. When I heard the call to ministry, I had heard only an occasional mention of Uncle Elmer. Ministry was not looked down on in the family; it just wasn't looked at much at all.

Nor was cancer considered something to worry about. It just wasn't a part of the family consciousness. Before me, there was no one in any generation who'd had cancer before the age of 80, and then only my Grandmother Pond, when she was 84, and Aunt Virginia, my mother's oldest sister, who got it when she was 80 and lived on into her 90s.

Granted, baldness was different. It was definitely in the family. My father was bald from his 20s. I was assured, however, that baldness skipped generations. I pointed out that my father's father preceded, and even exceeded him in domeness. That didn't look like a skipped generation. So I was assured that baldness was passed along from the mother's side, not the father's. Thus, I assumed I would have a beautiful mane of swept silver hair, like Bishop Richard Raines, upon my death bed.

It was no small adjustment in identity when the clearing began to appear on the back of my top.

I'm tall, and I was still wearing a flat-top, so the offending patch of pale wasn't highly visible at first. Hair then was short enough so that a lot of scalp showed anyway. Fortunately, in the early 1960s, long, or at least longer, hair became unfashionably fashionable. "Long-hairs" were suspected of playing the violin or of leftist leanings—the longer the hair, the lefter the lean. I had been labeled by Marie as a liberal long before and wasn't much bothered by a leftist tag, especially if it would cover up my growing forehead. I was considerably more interested in covering up the bald spot than in hiding any Christian tendencies that might have made me more socially compassionate than was acceptable.

I was sure that if I grew out my hair, I could comb it over, or around, or up, or directionally somehow, to cover that gleaming badge of aging. But if I grew it out, people would notice and realize what I was trying to do and make fun of me, which would defeat the whole notion of calling attention away from the infertility of my follicles.

Then I hit on a brilliant plan! Grow a beard at the same time! If long hair was leftist, beards were downright Communist. I mean, they were diabolical, evil, the exact opposite of Jesus himself, who surely must have used a Gillette double-edge every day.

The plan worked to perfection. As soon as I began to grow the beard, my friends ridiculed me, and my enemies excoriated me. They were so fixated on that beard, they didn't even notice what was happening up above it.

The only problem was the mirror. I had to spend a lot of time in front of it. Growing the hair out, combing it so it would cover the bald spot, trimming the beard, shaving the neck—way too much mirror time. I'd always gotten by with ignoring my crew cut entirely and swiping a razor quickly across the rest of my face. Not much mirror time there. Not much time to see my own face. Now it was in front of me all the time, and I didn't much like what I saw.

One day I was working away in front of the mirror when Helen passed by the open bathroom door.

"You know," I said, "I really am not very good looking."

"That's right," she said, sailing by on her way to the basement with a basket of dirty clothes.

That was when I realized I had made my statement in order to get an entirely different reaction.

"Wait a minute," I cried, pursuing her down the hall. "You're not supposed to agree when I say things like that. You're my wife."

"Well," she said, "you're never very good-looking when you're only looking at yourself, but you're very handsome when you're looking at me."

Helen has always been the best theologian in the family.

the real
"⑤lick willie"

Willie Lee Williams was the best. He wasn't the first, or the last, but he was the best, and I've been taken by some great ones. It was 1969.

Willie Lee was a Negro, or else he was black—we were in between terms on our campus. He was from Mississippi. He was a Methodist. He was a student. He was a little old for a student, and looked it, but he had gotten started late, having served in the military and worked for a few years to support his younger brothers and sisters before he could start college.

He was on his way to Chicago for a meeting of a special task force of our denomination on race relations. It was the first time blacks and whites, Southerners and Northerners, of our church were going to sit down together and hammer out the policies that would make us a nonracist church. Despite being poor and black and from Mississippi, Willie Lee was on the task force. It was a momentous time.

He called the Methodist bishop of Mississippi by name. The bishop had given Willie Lee some money. It wasn't enough, however, to buy a plane ticket and pay for his expenses at the conference. That didn't surprise me. The bishop of Mississippi was known throughout the church to be especially negligent in matters of race relations. Not actively racist, just willing to ignore the whole issue. To preserve his money, Willie Lee had hitchhiked most of the way. He had gotten as far as Bloomington, Illinois, that way, and he'd had some lonely and scary times, but mostly it hadn't been too bad. But then he had to catch a plane to get there in time for the meeting, which started early the next morning.

He had come to campus, knowing he could get help from his Methodist brothers and sisters at the Wesley

Foundation, knowing his race would not be held against him there. But before he had gotten to our building, he had passed the Black Cultural Center two doors down from us. He was very impressed that we had a black cultural center, so he had stopped in and talked to the folks there. He named them—the director and the secretary and some of the students. They had been so impressed with his mission, they had given him some money from their meager funds, even though he had not asked. Then he had passed the office of the Episcopal campus minister. He named him, talked about him. He had also given Willie Lee some money. Now, since Willie Lee was a Methodist, he was counting on his Methodist campus minister to provide the rest of the money for him.

I've been the victim of con artists plenty of times; every minister has. So I tried to ask the questions that would sort him out. Looking back, I realized that Willie knew every question before I did and provided an answer just before I could ask the question. It wasn't the answer I really needed, but it was enough that I couldn't ask the question. I thought about calling the Black Cultural Center or the Episcopal minister, but that would be rude, and we were definitely pressed for time.

The working day had almost passed away. It was less than an hour before the last plane to Chicago would be in the air. Willie needed "only" $45 more, which was not a small amount of money in those days. My secretary had gone home. I had no way to contact the treasurer of the Wesley Foundation and get a check from him and get it cashed before the bank would close and the plane would leave. I wasn't sure what line in the campus ministry budget I could pull money from for Willie Lee anyway. I piled Willie Lee into my car, caught the last minute of the last drive-up cashier at my bank, got Willie Lee the $45 out of my account, and drove him to the airport.

"Just enough time," he gasped, "to drop me in front," forestalling any intentions I may have had to park the car and see him off. He shook my hand, jumped from the car, and sprinted into the terminal.

I drove back to campus, feeling rather satisfied. It had been close, but Willie Lee, that poor black young man from Mississippi, was going to be at that meeting, and I had helped to make it possible. I decided to drop by the cultural center and the Episcopal campus ministry office so we could enjoy together the feeling of participating in a significant piece of ministry.

The secretary at the cultural center did not recognize Willie Lee by name; she didn't even recognize him by description.

"The man who got money for his trip to Chicago," I told her.

"Nobody got any money in here today," she replied.

"Well, not from you, from the director."

"He's not been in all day," she said. "Some black guy came in for just a second, but I was talking on the phone, so he just picked up one of those brochures off that table inside the door and left."

I picked up a brochure. In it were listed the names of the student steering committee of the center, the student names Willie Lee had mentioned to me. The director's name was on it, too. The secretary's name was on a plaque on her desk.

I walked over to the Episcopal campus ministry office. No, no black man had been there, and Nick, the minister, hadn't been in all afternoon. I walked out the door and saw Nick's name on the signboard out front.

It began to come clear. I'd been his target all along. He had just gathered information along the way that he could use in his tale of need. Willie Lee had played me with a story that he knew would gain him sympathy. He had fed me names he could get off brochures and signboards but knew I would recognize and trust. He may well have been from

Mississippi, and that may have been how he knew the name of the bishop there. It would not have surprised me, though, if his luggage consisted entirely of some handbook of denominations, listing all the officers of every church. Willie Lee was Methodist when it suited his purposes, but Baptist or Presbyterian or whatever when that would serve his plan better.

When Harry Golden ran a hotel in New York, he had one permanent resident who was a church prostitute. She went from church conference to church conference, plying her trade. "No high rollers," she said, "but it's safe, and I get to spend my time with nice people." He once asked her how she got customers at a church conference, and she had answered, "I just sit in the lobby, and they find me." She was a fount of information, always knowing before anyone else which denominations would merge, who would be elected bishop or moderator or president, how a conference would vote on any issue.

I think Willie Lee was like that. He worked churches because it was safe—and easy—and he got to spend time with nice—and naive—people. I'll bet he could have told you who'd be elected bishop, too.

I told the Wesley Foundation students the story of Willie Lee and what they had missed—the slickest con man in the game. If there's a hall of fame for such artists, Willie Lee must have a wall all his own. The students felt sorry for my loss. They put a can on the kitchen counter, labeled "The Willie Lee Williams Fund," to collect donations to defray my stupidity. They didn't feel *real* sorry for me; the can collected $1.43 over the rest of the school year. Of course, it's always possible there was much more, but Willie Lee returned from time to time, saw his name on the can, and kept helping himself.

"those who came to hear the word of God may ⓢtay."

"Do you know who Bob Harrington is?"

It was 11 o'clock on a Tuesday night in February. I had one foot in bed and one hand on the telephone. The voice in the phone belonged to my good friend, The Reverend Doctor William Luther White, a.k.a. Bill, the chaplain at Illinois Wesleyan University (IWU).

"Yes, I think so. He's the guy they call 'The Chaplain of Bourbon Street,' isn't he?"

"That's the one. A freelance pastor in 'The Quarter' in New Orleans. Quite a celebrity himself. Appears on TV a lot. He's a high-profile evangelical, and the more conservative students here were all over me to get him to come to preach in chapel. He's scheduled for 11 o'clock tomorrow, but his secretary just called and said he isn't coming. I asked if he were sick, and she said, no, he isn't, but he received another invitation, and he decided to go there instead. I can't believe it! He backs out, just 12 hours before he's scheduled! Those students who wanted him so badly are going to be really disappointed. They even have a special breakfast scheduled with him. And we've advertised him all over the state. He's so well known and popular, there are busloads of people from churches coming in here tomorrow!"

I began to get a strange feeling. I pulled my foot out of bed.

"You're in sort of a bind, aren't you?"

"Yes, I am, and I've got a really big favor to ask of you. Can you come preach in chapel tomorrow? After all, you're 'The Chaplain of Franklin Street.'"

Franklin Street ran for all of a mile between the campuses of IWU and Illinois State University, where I was the Wesley Foundation minister. I had never before been called "The Chaplain of Franklin Street." I've never heard that designation again, either, come to think of it.

I was young and ignorant and assumed I could do anything, especially when it came to preaching. Besides, Bill is my friend; you take chances, including the chance of looking foolish, for your friends. And there were those busloads of Baptists and campus conservatives to impress, too.

"You want me to come for breakfast, too?"

"No, I don't think so. Even I wasn't invited to that. That was just going to be Bob and the students. Now I'll have to go and explain to them."

Just as well; more time to prepare for whatever I was going to do. Then I realized I needed sleep more than I needed to think through what I would say. I needed to prepare the preacher, not the sermon. I had spent many years preparing the preacher's brain and spirit, preparing myself to know the Story and be able to tell it in such a way that those listening could find themselves in it. Now I needed to go to sleep and trust God and the Story to be there when I awoke and stepped into the pulpit at IWU's chapel service.

IWU didn't have a chapel building in those days. Services were held in the auditorium of the music building. It, however, was undergoing renovations, so chapel that year took place in the ballroom of the Union Building, with many rows of brown metal folding chairs stretching from one wall to the other, and a small, low platform to one side.

Every chair was full. Student ushers were carrying in even more chairs and putting them wherever there was a square or two of unoccupied ballroom linoleum. People had to crane their necks around the rows of heads in front of them to see the platform. On that platform were a piano, two more folding chairs, and a podium.

Bill and I walked out of the doors right behind the platform, promptly at 11, as the piano played a prelude, walked
out of the doors from the ballroom kitchen, and sat on the
two folding chairs. I wore my double-breasted blue blazer,
gray shirt and slacks, silver and black rep tie—very wide. I
sported big reddish-blond fuzzy sideburns and matching
mustache and goatee. I must have looked at least a little bit
like what people would expect of "The Chaplain of Bourbon
Street."

"How did breakfast go?" I asked him.

"Not too well. They were badly disappointed. They're
not even here."

That should have been a signal to me; it wasn't.

The ushers had passed out bulletins listing the events
and the players in the service. The bulletins had been prepared, of course, before Bill knew he needed to list a
pinch-hitter; Bob Harrington's name was still there. We
went through the first part of the service—hymns, prayers,
litanies, scripture readings. Then it came time for the
preacher.

Bill arose and explained the situation as best he could,
trying to be as gracious as possible, under the circumstances,
toward the missing chapel preacher. People began to get
restless. He started to explain that they were fortunate,
because he'd been able to get another preacher on very short
notice.

I don't know exactly what I had expected. I knew many
people would be disappointed, maybe slump down into
their seats, mutter to their neighbors, then shut up and listen. After all, they'd come to a chapel service. That wasn't
what happened.

They got up and left. Simply stood up, grumbling, shov-
ing chairs out of the way, not trying at all to be quiet about
their exit, throwing nasty looks at me, as though it were my
fault that I was not Bob Harrington. They didn't even wait
to find out who I was. People who had come a hundred

miles on a school bus were willing to let that bone-rattling ride amount to nothing, not even invest 20 more minutes to see if maybe God had something to say through a hair-rimmed mouth they had, up until that very moment, been looking forward to listening to when they thought it belonged to someone else.

I remembered a story I had read about Arthur Beecher, one of Rev. and Mrs. Lyman Beecher's seven remarkable children, including Harriet Beecher Stowe, and one of the most famous preachers ever, Henry Ward Beecher. Arthur was a preacher, too. For a Sunday when Henry had to be absent from the Brooklyn pulpit he had made famous, or notorious, according to one's view, Arthur had been summoned down from Elmira to do the preaching. When he was announced, many in the congregation got up and began to leave. Arthur jumped to the pulpit and called out, "Those of you who came to hear Henry Ward Beecher may leave. Those who came to hear the Word of God may stay." They returned to their seats.[1]

I thought about pulling an Arthur—I really did. The only problem was, I wasn't sure what that congregation was going to hear, so I wasn't about to proclaim that it was the Word of God until I'd had a chance to hear it myself.

Bill waited until they had cleared the hall, and then introduced me. Maybe 75 people remained . . . some embarrassed-looking IWU faculty, students who came every week to chapel—regardless of who was preaching—and some townfolk who did the same. They were scattered around a ballroom that now looked like it had suffered an especially uninspiring prom night.

The scriptural text was 1 John 4:7-12. I told stories. I think it was a pretty good sermon. At least, *I* must have liked it. My notes show that, following the impromptu chapel appearance, I preached it 14 times over nine years, under four different titles. I have preached only one other sermon more than that.

Several people approached me after the service to thank me for coming, and to apologize for the exodus. One young woman, a sophomore or junior, I would guess, said simply, "I came to hear Bob Harrington, too. I'm so glad he didn't come." I was glad, too. His absence taught me to learn to trust the Story to carry the sermon where it needs to go.

note

[1]Arthur was a remarkable man. He was summoned to his church in Elmira on a one-month call (hired for one month), and stayed for 37 years, on one-month calls. Can you imagine being voted on every month for 37 years? The first month he was there he was thrown out of the ministerial association for heresy. Thereafter, he never missed a meeting of the association in all his 37 years, even though he was never readmitted to membership.

"i never did agree
with Jesus on that one"

Unlike commentators and talk show hosts, the preacher doesn't get to spew out anything she or he wants and claim that it's truth. The truth, Christians claim, is revealed in the Bible. We have to use experience (Does this speak to my spirit?) and reason (Does this speak to my mind?) and tradition (Does this speak the same "at all times and in all places?") in interpreting the Scriptures, but the Bible is the plumb line and the baseline. From a preaching point of view, it is supposed to keep us from arrogance.

Because the Bible is the plumb line and baseline, it is often referred to as the "Word of God," God's communication with us. The Bible, however, is not the Word of God. For Christians, Christ, not the Bible, is the Word of God. It's basically a 20th-century phenomenon, this equation of Bible with Word of God. I'm not exactly sure why so many people are beguiled by this notion in our day. I suspect, however, it is because the way of Jesus is difficult and unpopular. From a preacher's point of view, Jesus is hard to preach. Doing so gets us into all sorts of troubles. The Bible, however, is such a wondrously broad book that we can always find something in it somewhere to allow us to add some artificial sweetener to the way of Jesus and make it more palatable. Strangely, adherence to the Bible doesn't save us from arrogance, but creates it. Look out when a preacher, or anyone else, starts a sentence with, "The Bible says . . ." That's when you're going to hear what *the preacher* says.

The Bible is the rule by which all other forms of revelation are measured, because it is the song in which the Christ spirit and the Christ story are sung in the world and in the church and in the hearts of individuals. It is no more the Word of God, though, than was the donkey that carried

Jesus into Jerusalem on Palm Sunday. The donkey was, and the Bible is, a vehicle for the Word of God. Nonetheless, the Bible is the Rolls Royce of vehicles, the final authority for judging words to see if they partake of the Word. If you can hear anything but the clock, it's not biblical truth.[1]

There is great danger for the preacher, and for the congregation, if what is thrown out from the pulpit is not "biblical." Not surprisingly, then, the Bible is the great stone of stumbling for preachers. Without arrogance, it is very rare that a preacher can claim that she or he is interpreting the Bible with accurate precision. We are required, however, to stand up every seven days and act like we have something to say, and it's supposed to be "biblical." So, dangerously we speak what we hope is biblical truth, what we want to be biblical truth, but which is more likely to be the mirror of our own fears and struggles.

But being unfaithful to the Bible is only the start of the danger. What if we are *faithful* to it? What if we do speak biblical truth? Jesus is the Christ, and Christ is the Word of God, which by definition is the truth, and we all know what happened to Jesus! It's not a far stretch to guess what will happen to us if we preach the same truth he did.

During the 1960s my friend, Walt Wagener, was the Wesley Foundation minister at a small state university in a small town. The town itself had no black residents, and the university had only begun to admit black students. The town wasn't quite prepared for this, and a good deal of harassment of the few black students occurred. The harassers included the town police. One black young man, religiously inclined and also a poet, was arrested for one imagined infraction or another whenever he ventured off campus and into town.

From time to time Wesley Foundation students led the worship at the local Methodist church. For one service Walt invited the harassed young man to read some of his poetry in a worship service. All Hades broke loose, masked by the worst racism of all, the kind that proclaims it is not. In this case the protesters claimed they were not opposed to his participation in worship because he was black, but because he was "a convicted felon," stemming from his various arrests in town.

One member of the church called the chairman of the Wesley Foundation board of directors—the dean of the college and a member of the church—to protest. Instead of taking on the racial issues directly, the dean reminded his caller that Jesus was especially open and kindly to those who were marginal in society, including those on the wrong side of the law.

"Well, then," said the man, "I'll just go over to Milwaukee and get some whore prostitute to come over here and read her poetry in worship. What do you think about that?"

The dean allowed as how that would probably be in keeping with Christian worship, since Jesus had forgiven the woman caught in adultery. There was a long pause. Then the man said, "Well, I never did agree with Jesus on that one."

Most people aren't that honest. They don't agree with Jesus, especially about accepting the unacceptable, but it's hard to come right out and say Jesus is wrong. It's much easier, when we want to disagree with Jesus, to take it out on the preacher and to hide behind the Bible.

The Bible is dangerous, to the preacher and to the congregation, whether it's preached well or poorly.

note

[1]Before the days of digital timepieces, when clocks still ran clockwise, Rolls Royce advertised that its cars were built so well that all you could hear was the ticking of the clock.

the d@ring young man in the flying pulpit

My wife slipped into her accustomed pew. She was young, didn't look much older than the many college girls who came to worship there. In a church that herded more than a thousand worshipers in and out of four services each Sunday morning, she certainly wasn't recognizable as "the preacher's wife," especially since she was the newest of three such creatures. Her husband was the campus minister, and most of the "real people who live in the real world" in the congregation weren't sure that someone who spent most of his time working with students ought to be considered a minister anyway. Thus, the couple who tromped into the pew just in front of her had no idea who was overhearing their conversation.

The man opened his bulletin. "Good grief! McFarland's preaching," he stage-whispered to his wife.

"Let's leave," she replied, her nose wrinkled as though sniffing something out in Denmark.

They left, but not without the young woman in the row behind them seriously considering sticking out a foot to trip them.

Almost 30 years after that couple walked out before they heard what I might have to say, I spoke at the 40th anniversary of my high school class. Late in the evening Bob Robling and I were chatting.

"You remember that summer after our freshman year in college?" he asked. "Dave Lamb and Don Taylor and Bob Wallace and you and I went around to little churches all summer while pastors were on vacation, and we'd sing as a quartet and you'd preach."

I remembered that summer and those friends with great affection and no small amount of wonderment. It was at the end of that summer that I had told the District Superintendent I was called to ministry. It was at the end of that summer that he sent me to Chrisney.

"I've often told people," Bob went on, "that the best preacher I ever heard was an 18-year-old kid."

That anonymous couple and my friend Bob are the poles between which preachers fly—not magnetic poles, but the poles that hold up the flying trapeze called the pulpit. On one side are aerial catchers who don't even want you in the act. On the other side are those who think you're so good, they don't need to worry about you. One bunch is probably as dangerous to you as the other, since one is as likely as the other to ignore your cries for help. But when the time comes to let go of the bar and preach, you still feel better launching yourself out into the air toward those who say you're the best preacher they've ever heard.

Every year for a preacher is a year of preaching dangerously, even if she or he doesn't mean to. There is danger either for the preacher or for the congregation. In good years there is danger for both.

Preaching is dangerous by its very nature. If a preacher is honest to God, she or he is facing off against the conventional wisdom. It is dangerous because people might not understand you. It is dangerous because they might understand you.

I have said remarkably little about preaching anywhere else in these pages, even though it is one of the central tasks of ministry and has been the focus of a great deal of my work and study. There are two reasons for that:

(1) It's just hard. Anyone who's ever read anything about language theory knows how the very process of trying to talk about talk twists the talker into a pretzel. It's hard because any use of language—especially preaching, I think—is a unified action. To talk about it, we have to break it down into unnatural parts.

I find it helpful to say that preaching moves from story (event) to theory and back to story (experience), from story to concept and back to story. It starts and ends with story. The preacher tells God's story in such a way that the listener can see his or her story as part of God's narrative. The listener processes that in thought, even though it may be very elemental thought, and then moves onto more story, more experience, more life. That starts the process over again. Those movements, however, are layered and tangled, like clothes in a dryer, not strung out distinctly, one by one, like clothes on a line. It's more like a complex weaving than a string of beads.

Basically, all the preacher can do is to throw the story of life, the story of God, the story of love, into the air and hope that someone says, "Aha, that's mine," and reaches out to grab it.

(2) Preaching is like eating. I've eaten 64,605 meals in my life, not counting snacks. I probably couldn't describe more than 10 of them to you in any detail. But because I can't remember them doesn't mean they weren't important to me, that they didn't nourish me, that I could have gotten along without them.

I'm sometimes amazed when I run into a parishioner from a former church and that person will tell me in detail about a sermon I preached 20 or 30 years before. She remembers it much better than I. Indeed, sometimes I can't remember it at all. I've never had the courage, however, to ask if she could remember any other sermon I preached in the years I was her pastor. The one she remembers met a special need at a particular time. It was pivotal for her in some way. That doesn't mean the others she heard weren't helpful; they just didn't open any doorways toward God. Still, if we talk about sermons past, it will be a short conversation.

My wife says I shouldn't worry so much about finding some new way to throw the story out into the air each week, some new way that will cause my listeners to look up and grab it before it falls onto their heads with a thud.

"You really have only one thing to do," she says. "That's to remind us that God loves us."

That's a good definition of good preaching.

Of course, it reminds me of the story of the preacher who was making his retirement speech at the annual conference.

"Those of you who have heard me preach over the years will be aware that I really only had two themes through all that time," he said.

One of his colleagues turned to his neighbor and said, "You mean there was a second?"

No, if he were preaching well, there was not a second. There's only one. But there are 64,605 ways of throwing it out into the air.[1]

note

[1] It's a dangerous thing for preachers to mention numbers and lists. One preacher is said to have noted in a sermon that there were 435 different sins, and was promptly besieged for copies of the list.

"don't c@ll me 'Bill!'"

I can't quite recall now why I wanted that Ph.D. so badly. It is a research and teaching degree. I like to teach, and most folks say I'm a natural at it. I never really felt called to teach, though, not as a profession, and I certainly have never liked that necessary duty of classroom teaching—assigning grades. One doesn't need a Ph.D. to be a good minister. If you're not sure of your call to pastoral ministry, however, you look with longing at the groves of academia and begin to see all sorts of beauty in ivy that you cannot see in stained glass.

Being a campus minister, I was around tweedy doctored types all the time. They fell into two camps: those who insisted on being called "Doctor," and those who wiped their glasses with carefully pressed red bandannas and mumbled, "Aw, you don't need to call me doctor." I liked the folks in the latter group better. I wanted to be one of them. You can't be that humble about your doctorate if there's no chance of anyone calling you "Doctor" anyway.

Also, from my first year at Indiana University, I knew that the Ph.D. was as far as you could go. I don't like to stop partway to anything.

Whatever the reason, there I was, at the age of 35, with a Danforth Fellowship in hand to pay my way, trying to get a Ph.D. behind my name. Maybe it was on the off-chance that I might need it someday. Maybe it was because I had just always assumed I would do it. Regardless, I knew that if I were going to do it at all, it had to be before I started paying for my children to go to college.

So there I was, a student in the School of Religion at the University of Iowa, trying to get a Ph.D., in a process I have often likened to a hurdle race for a one-legged person. The faculty doesn't care how you manage the hurdles or in what order you do them. You just have to limp up to each one, climb over it or knock it down, then drag it off the track and get a dozen folks who otherwise aren't paying any attention to take out their knives and carve their initials in it.

I was in the graduate student lounge that afternoon, getting my leg limbered up for one of the biggest of the hurdles. It was an off-day for most, so I was the only person in the lounge, or at least I thought I was. This hurdle, like most of them, was hard reading. I was concentrating, trying to focus, getting ready for qualifying exams. Then I sensed an alien presence. I looked up. *Bill was standing in the doorway.

I couldn't remember ever having seen him in the grad students' lounge before, but I knew him fairly well. I'd never had a class with him, though, and never would. My fields were theology and church history and pastoral care. I was working specifically on the relationship between communication theory and theological method. He taught in an entirely different field. I thought of him as a peer. We were both in our mid-30s, both ordained ministers in the same denominational body, where we had equal status and equal votes. Almost all my contacts with him were outside the university—at church functions, at parties, at departmental gatherings in bars, where he and I were the cola drinkers.

"You really managed to mess things up," he said, his voice choking a little when he got to "mess."

I knew what he was talking about, of course. I was anticipating some sort of response, but still I was surprised at his abruptness.

The dates for the qualifying exams had been scheduled long ago. Those of us who were taking them that year had worked hard, getting ready, trying to peak our knowledge and our energy at the right time.

Bill, however, had been negotiating with an important figure in his field of study to come for a special series of lectures. Shortly before qualifiers, he learned that the dates for which the lecturer could come were the same as the exams.

Bill didn't want anything else interfering with the special lectures, wanted to be sure all the faculty and students were able to come to them, so he asked the faculty to reschedule the qualifying exams for different dates. They did so. The grad students didn't know anything about it until we found a notice posted on the bulletin board in our lounge.

All the students were upset. It was inconvenient, at the least, to be rescheduled. Most of us were taking classes in addition to preparing for the qualifying exams. We had papers to write and exams to take for those courses, too. Most of us were teaching assistants and had lectures to give and papers to grade for the classes we taught. Most of us had families, who were already wondering why they never saw us. Several of us had other jobs, some serving as pastors of churches. Those work schedules couldn't be twisted around at short notice to accommodate the changed qualifying exam schedule. Some of us were on tight time schedules for our degrees, needing to complete that particular jump of the Ph.D. hurdle race in order to be in rhythm for the hurdles yet to come. It was also demeaning not to be consulted.

I was one of the oldest students, older than some of the faculty. I was used to being consulted about decisions that affected my life, used to negotiating. It seemed logical to me to tell the dean and the faculty how we felt about this rescheduling, especially since none of the students taking the exams had planned to go to the lectures anyway.

I did so. The dean agreed. He took the matter to the faculty. They reversed their decision. The qualifying exams and the lectures would take place at the same time. I had heard that Bill wasn't happy about it, but I hadn't seen him since the original exam dates had been reinstated.

"You really managed to mess things up." He went on to tell of all the work he had put into getting the special lecturer, how important the man was, how I had deprived some students of the singular opportunity to hear him, how inappropriate it was for a graduate student to question a decision of the faculty. Unspoken was his embarrassment at having his request overruled at the request of a mere grad student.

I was surprised that he seemed to understand so little about how important the qualifying exams were to us, how busy our schedules were, how peripheral a special lecture in a different field was to our lives and goals. I started to explain.

"Well, Bill . . ."

That was as far as I got. His face turned red. I could hear his teeth grind. The veins in his neck bulged out.

"Don't call me 'Bill!'" he growled. "We're not on a first-name basis. I'm a Ph.D. You're not. You're a student, just a student. You run around here, messing things up, acting like you've earned it. Well, you haven't. When you've got your doctorate, then you can call me 'Bill.'"

I was caught totally off guard. I hadn't expected anything like that. Angry with me for "messing up" his plans? Sure, I could understand that, and I was ready to respond to it. But so much hostility just because I had called him by his first name? Did he really think people should call him "Dr. *Bortz" all the time, never call him by his first name? No, I'd heard many people call him "Bill," and he'd never asked them not to do it. I'd done it myself a dozen times before, in a church basement, in the living room of some professor's house, at the tavern where grad students and profs gathered on Thursday nights.

I don't think I called him anything right then, though. I just apologized.

"I'm sorry," I said. "I didn't mean to be offensive. It won't happen again."

Then his face turned cosmic. It was only red before. Now it was on fire. His tongue got thick, too, apparently, since he had trouble forcing words out around it.

"I didn't mean . . . not offensive . . . just . . . I mean . . . not offensive . . . first names . . ."

He turned on his heel and left, leaving a cloud of confused hostility, a cloud the size of a man's doctorate. I sat there, staring at the empty place where he had been. What was that all about? Why had he gotten so worked up about me calling him by his first name and then was so embarrassed when I apologized? Wasn't that what he wanted? When he tried to pull his words back, tried to do his own apology for making me apologize, he said I hadn't been offensive. But if he hadn't thought it was offensive for me to call him by his first name, why did he get so excited about it?

Well, at least I didn't have to offer an explanation to him about the schedule for the exams. I could go back to studying. I opened up again the thick and dusty book I had been reading.

The words on the page turned fuzzy, though. My brain kept going back to Bill, or Dr. Bortz, or Herr Professor, or whoever he was. My brain began to get mad. The nerve of ...! If he didn't want to be called by his first name by a mere grad student, he should have told me so the first time I called him Bill. Who did he think he was to treat me like that, just because he had a doctorate? We were fellow clergy members of the same denominational body. Most importantly, we were fellow Christians, a faith in which status distinctions are not supposed to be noticed, let alone counted.

The more I thought about it, the madder I got. I paced around the lounge enough to slosh old coffee in the cups on the table. Then I launched myself out of the building, across the campus, across the river, up into the office of David Belgum, another professor in our department.

I told him of my encounter with Bill, of what he had said, of how angry I was.

"I just don't understand it, Dave ..."

Then I heard myself doing it again. This man was *not* a peer. He was 20 years my senior, a fellow clergyman, to be sure, but in another denomination, a much more formal denomination. He was a distinguished writer of books and an acclaimed expert in his field of pastoral care and counseling, a full professor, one of *my* professors, one who would give me a qualifying exam the next week, on schedule. Here I was calling him by his first name, as I had done many times before. It was my turn again to apologize.

"I'm sorry. I've been calling you by your first name all this time, and I've never asked you about it. Maybe you don't think that's appropriate, either."

"Well, I've been around a long time," he said. "I've found that whatever people call me is what they need to call me. Some call me 'Pastor'; they need me right then in my religious role. Some call me 'Professor'; they're relating to me as a teacher. Some call me 'Mister'; it's a business role, maybe when I take the car to the garage. Some call me 'Dave'; they're relating to me as a friend. Some can't make up their minds, and use a hybrid, like 'Pastor Dave.' I listen to what folks call me, and I respond to that. I think that's important as a minister. Listen carefully to how people address you, and you'll have an idea right off what they need from you. You'll do better pastoral care if you don't tell people what to call you, but let them take the lead."

Some ministers tell people what to call them. Especially popular in recent times has been the first name coupled with the pastoral title. "Just call me 'Reverend Julie.' " "Just call me 'Father Todd.' " I guess it's meant to split the difference, provide some distinction while at the same time informing you that the status-holder is just a regular guy or gal. It still keeps the minister in the position of telling the other person what the relationship must be instead of listening for what the other person needs. In that way it's not much different from "Don't call me 'Bill.' "

Yes, I wanted that Ph.D. for a similar reason, so I could say to lesser beings, to show what a regular and humble fellow I was, while still reminding them of my advanced status,

"Oh, don't call me 'Doctor.'" It's the exact opposite of "Don't call me 'Bill,'" but it's still the same.

"we gave you a ©hance"

I knew I shouldn't eat three hot-dogs, but they tasted so good, so full, as we sat on a bale of hay under a harvest moon beside the roasting fire in the *Jacksons' big backyard.

I chased the three hot-dogs down with three s'mores. To create a s'more, you first toast a marshmallow, burned black on the outside, still cold and gooey white on the inside, just the way God wrote the recipe. Then you put it between two graham crackers, along with half a chocolate bar, and eat it. It's so good, you ask for s'more.

The fire was a bit too hot, the wind from the wrong direction, as they always are at wiener roasts, but the heat of that fire on my face was the warmth of contentment. It had been a long time since we'd had friends with whom we felt so much at home. We'd never had such close friends within a congregation before. It felt so good, I didn't notice that the warmth on my face was countered by a chill October breeze on my neck.

Everything seemed so natural. The Jacksons were a loving family. They had sons the same age as our daughters. The kids all got along great. *Ken and *Wilma were ideal church members—active, personable, outgoing.

Best of all, they really liked us, just as people—or so it seemed. We hardly ever talked about the church when we were together. We traded ideas on raising children, worried together about how to pay for their college educations, wondered how best to care for aging parents. We were just friends. I even went to the discount store and bought a pair of heavy work shoes so I could use my day off to help Ken cut firewood.

Then the day came that they telephoned and asked for an appointment to see me in my office at the church building. It was very formal. I feared the worst. Every pastor knows "ideal" families who cover up physical or mental or sexual abuse. Every pastor knows "perfect" marriages that come apart faster than a butcher can cleave a steak. I feared the worst.

It was the worst, but not the "worst" I had feared.

They walked into my office silently, almost sullenly, their eyes following the weave pattern in my rug. They sat side by side and very straight on the chairs that churches buy from the "Discomfort Furniture" catalog.

"When you came here to pastor," Ken said, "we decided to give you a chance. We had already thought about going to the Community Evangelical Church over in *Oswald, because this church really isn't strict enough. We want our boys to be brought up without a lot of bad influences. We thought maybe you'd be different. We decided we'd take a real close look at you. We gave you a chance, but you failed."

They got up, stiffly and strictly, and walked out. They never came back.

"i just came
to watch you work."

The stroke hit *Fred only nine days after we moved to town. My predecessor, Reverend Wonderful (this is always the name of your predecessor for the first few months, or years, you are on the job) knew Fred well; he had pastored him for nine years. There's a big difference between nine years and nine days. I hadn't even met Fred yet. But Reverend Wonderful wasn't there. I was Fred's pastor.

On the face of it, Reverend Wonderful probably couldn't have done much better at pastoring Fred then than I did. The stroke was massive. Fred was comatose, his watery eyes sometimes open, but staring blankly, whitely. He lay in his hospital bed, curled up, a small man made even smaller by the fetal position, preparing to exit this life much as he had entered it 80 years before. After a few days his family stopped going to the hospital. I, a stranger, was his only regular visitor.

With comatose patients the conventional and helpful wisdom is this: "You never know . . ." You never know if comatose persons can hear you, or how much, or if they understand. It's possible that they hear, that they hear a lot, that they understand what you are saying to them and about them. If not, it's still possible that they recognize voices, even if they don't put meaning to the words. You never know but that person in the bed might be comforted simply by the sound of your voice.

I have a comforting voice. After a funeral, one distant relative, having heard me for the first time, said, "He could recite the alphabet and make you feel better." My voice isn't something I've developed, nothing for which I can take credit. It's just there, the legacy of my father and his father before him. I sometimes suspect that a person with a pleasant voice, especially a man, confuses that gift with a call to ministry. For all its comfortableness, though, mine was still a voice Fred had never heard. Three times a week I entered Fred's room and used my voice, but not my ears. It was the same monologue each time.

"Hello, Fred. This is Reverend (as a minister, you never refer to yourself as "Doctor" in a hospital setting) McFarland again, the new pastor at your church. We didn't meet before you came to the hospital. Do you remember Reverend Wonderful? I replaced him. He'd come to see you if he were still here. I've told him about you, so he can pray for you. All the people at church are praying for you. Your family says 'Hello.' We had a nice crowd at church Sunday, even though it was an awfully hot day. Good corn-growing weather, though, isn't it? That's what we always say to make this hot weather bearable."

Then I would hold his limp, dry hand and pray.

"God, this is Fred and me again. We're doing our best. Stay with us, please. Help us to get through each day. We don't understand, but we trust you . . ."

Days stretched to weeks that yielded to months. The only thing that changed was the terrain.

"Hello, Fred. This is Reverend McFarland, the new pastor, again. Remember me? . . . The leaves are turning. About half the crop is in . . ."

"God, this is Fred and me again . . ."

One deep autumn day a student nurse followed me into Fred's room. She was so quiet, stepping softly on brand new, thick-soled nurse shoes, that I didn't notice her until I got to Fred's bed and turned around. She stood small against the wall, hands clasped respectfully in front of her over the blue uniform apron that marked her as a novice, the heavy stethoscope hanging around her neck and clear down to her waist. I stepped back to let her try out her new stethoscope, or pull at the sheets, or do whatever she had come to do.

She didn't move from her place. We stood there awkwardly for a moment.

"I won't get in your way," I said.

"Oh, no," she replied, perkily, but still respectfully. "It's a class assignment. I just came to watch you work."

Work? Work? I wasn't working, not in the way everyone else in the hospital worked. I mean, I wasn't *doing* anything. You can watch a nurse work, or a surgeon, or an x-ray technician, or the cook. You can't watch a minister work, not in a hospital. I was just representing the faith and the church, trying to remind a comatose man that in the company of those twin strangers called life and death, he wasn't alone, that God loved him, even now, perhaps especially now.

If I'd had a blood vial or a stethoscope . . . If I'd even had a patient who could talk back . . . then maybe she could watch me work. Just to listen to a pastor talk to himself . . . I felt stupid enough, going through this routine each visit, knowing full well, despite the conventional wisdom, that this was wasted time, agreeing with the absence of Fred's family. But with an audience . . .

"Hello, Fred. This is Reverend McFarland. I'm still the new pastor . . ."

It was all I had to do, to show her how a minister works in the hospital, to give her something to write up for her teacher, so she and her classmates could laugh about how ridiculous and irrelevant it is to have pastors wandering into hospital rooms, talking to comatose stroke victims just like they are normal folk, taking up time and space that could be better used by the real workers, those with the forward scopes around their necks instead of the backward collars.

"God, this is Fred and me again . . ."

I let go of Fred's hand and turned to go, ready to mumble an apology for not putting on a better show. She stood with the end of the stethoscope pressed against her own heart. Tears ran down her seamless cheeks.

"Thank you for letting me watch you work," she whispered. Then she turned and scurried out.

She'd be about 45 now. I'm sure she's a head nurse somewhere. I'd like to watch her work.

moving in

I don't remember now who it was who came to get me. I suppose that's not surprising. There were only a few persons in town I could recognize, those on the Pastor-Parish Relations (Personnel) Committee, the ones who had interviewed me a month before. I hadn't met anyone else yet. It was, after all, move-in day.

I was standing behind the moving van, under a big oak tree, chatting with the movers. It was lunchtime. The van was about half-empty now. Women from the church had brought us a casserole and fresh rolls. I was inviting the moving men to have lunch with us when a man in a suit drove up and parked under the other oak and approached us.

He hesitated. I was dressed in a t-shirt and jeans. So were the movers. He wasn't sure which one was the new pastor.

I'd been through a lot of moves by then, though. I could spot a church member, even if I'd never seen him before, come ostensibly to welcome the new pastor, but really to check him out. I stuck out my hand and introduced myself.

He didn't hesitate anymore, just blurted it out.

"The high school principal's wife just died. Out at the local hospital. Only 48. Never been sick before. Just got to feeling bad last night. Took her out to the hospital. Just died. Family's waiting at the house . . ."

"They're waiting for you." I'd heard that phrase first at Chrisney and dozens of times since then. It didn't make any difference that we'd never met, that the pastor they knew and trusted had moved out just the day before. I was there. Move-in day or not, I was the pastor.

I didn't know my way around town. I asked the man to wait so he could lead me to the house. The movers said they'd find the rest of the wardrobe boxes and carry them up to our bedroom. I trotted into the house and told Helen. She found a towel and washcloth and sent me into the bathroom to wipe off some of the moving grime. By the time I was out, she'd found a blue suit and a white shirt in one of the wardrobe boxes.

If I'd been there a while, knew those folks, already been seen in a suit or robe, I would have gone as I'd been found, in jeans and t-shirt. When you are an unknown quantity, though, you need to identify yourself by the symbols you wear on your body.

The man led me to the house, pointed it out with a wave of his arm, and drove on. I rang the doorbell and then explained to a middle-aged woman who I was. She was a neighbor. She brought me inside, left me standing at the door of the living room while she went to get the new widower, a grieving man who would be in charge of the education of my children. Several people stared at me, not unfriendly, but in grief, not remembering what to do when a stranger enters the house. I started around the room, as though I were the host, introducing myself as the new pastor, not asking for names or relationships, just letting them know I was there, letting them know that in me, the church was there.

The neighbor returned and took me to the kitchen. The widower sat there, drinking coffee, looking stunned.

"Cold," he told me. "That's how it feels . . . just cold."

There was more than grief, as it turned out. Guilt, too. They'd had a friend who had died at the local hospital. Inadequate care, they were sure. He and his wife had made a pact that they'd never put each other in that hospital, that they'd call an ambulance and send the other to the big hospital, 50 miles away.

"But it happened so fast," he said. "One minute she was okay, and then all of a sudden she was really sick. All I could think to do was get help as quick as possible. . . . Then she died, and I remembered what she'd said about this hospital."

He never mentioned his guilt to anyone else. He didn't need to. He'd never seen me before, but I was his pastor.

the t@ll-girl bride

I was 40 that year; 40 makes you age-conscious. I had started identifying people, yes, evaluating them, by their age.

He looked 50. I learned later that he was 37, 5'8", bald, and paunchy.

She looked 45. She was actually 25—25 years, 6', and 200 pounds of raw-boned hillbilly muscle. She wore old cowboy boots, lumpy black cord pants, and a dark green sweatshirt with a small bleach stain over her left breast. There was not a trace of makeup on her red face or an ounce of energy in her thin, lifeless hair.

I got them seated in the twin brown counseling chairs in front of my desk, then took my place behind it. A desk is a barrier. It adds psychological distance. A pastor should never raise up emotional barriers, even if they're scarred with time and their drawers won't shut. But I'd been around the counseling block a time or two. I'd learned to read faces and attitudes. I knew this couple wanted something from me that would take me places I did not want to go. I wanted that cheap veneer protection between me and them. I compromised by leaning back and putting my feet on it.

He sat as in a trance. She did the talking, but only to my battered beige carpet. She seemed to draw strength from it, a piece of cloth that had absorbed all the problems anyone could possibly spill out over it.

They wanted to get married. Naturally. People who should never marry, at least each other, always want to get married.

They weren't my responsibility, not members of my church. I had never seen either of them before.

"Why have you come to me?"

She sighed, and spoke to the carpet.

"They say, when there's no place else to go, people come to you."

Bingo! Hook set in the mouth of the "radical priest." They'd come to the Protestant patron of lost causes. I could just see my picture on a medal in her pocket.

What it really meant, of course, was that they'd already been to every other minister in town and been turned down. I knew that, but . . . I remembered the limerick. "She knew what it meant, but she went."

I tried to do all the things I had been taught in seminary and had learned since, tried to counsel them about the nature and meaning of marriage. None of it seemed to register on *Bernice or *Roland, or even on me for that matter. We talked about why they wanted to get married, about their hopes and fears, about his failed first marriage, about his children she would be raising.

I was fulfilling some vague ministerial mandate called "premarital counseling," trying to build up a defense against the unseen jury of my professors. Roland and Bernice thought I was just curious.

They both drove taxis. That was how they met. It was on breaks between runs that he had wooed and won her, as they sipped machine coffee in the garage or were parked next to each other at a taxi stand.

He needed someone to take care of his children. She had always wanted a family. There was no talk of love. Instead they spoke of how they would arrange their driving schedules.

He was getting a live-in babysitter and a second income. She was getting something six-foot girls with stringy hair and football figures hardly ever get—a proposal.

She did not want to spoil her only chance with too much talk.

She never looked up, at me or at her husband-to-be. Her eyes never wavered from the toes of her muddy boots, planted firmly on my napless rug. She was focused. She didn't want some preacher messing things up with educated talk about the meaning of love. She just wanted to get married.

Oh, not right away, of course. A week from Saturday, almost 10 days away. And wasn't it the funniest thing, that she was going to get married to a man whose last name was "Wedding." Yes, Roland *Wedding (The real name had the same meaning). She would get wed to Wedding on her wedding day. She seemed to think it was an omen. So did I.

They didn't want to wed in the church, though. He had been in church only once, when he married the first time. She had never been to church, nor had any member of her family. She was sure they would not know how to act—and so was I.

She wrote out directions to the house where she was spending her last few days as a child in her parents home. Then she stood to leave. She looked me in the eye for the first time. I'm six feet and an inch. She didn't have to look up to be eye to eye.

"Guess I'm gonna be the tallest bride you ever saw. Yeah, a tall-girl bride."

• • • • •

It was a good thing she'd written out the directions. In *Irish 80, the streets had names, but there were no signposts. The houses had numbers, but they weren't on the houses. Each home was remarkably different from its neighbors, far more so than the houses in some expensive suburb. To the outsider, though, they all just looked like shacks. The directions told me that the tireless, blocked-up '57 Chevy in the front yard was pink and blue.

I knew it would be a disaster. I was sure I was betraying my profession and my church. These people had no idea what the words in the wedding service meant. What did they understand of "holy estates, the fear of God, holy covenants, spiritual grace, pledging faith?" How could I justify being a part of this? Three months of counseling maybe? But they wanted to get married now. There were children to care for, taxis to drive.

They knew, and I knew, that I was the only person in town with the power to sign a marriage license who would actually do a wedding service for them. I was in too deep. The day came, and I went.

I would have called the "yard car" coral and aqua. Someone had painted it with a brush. She was standing in the front yard, waiting for me, even though it was one of those false, sunny, spring days when the temperature is in the 30s.

As I got out of my pastorly Ford station wagon, my eyes were at the level of her lace bodice. I knew the woman was tall, but good grief! She towered over me. She must have been wearing four-inch heels. I tried to check, but the hem of her gown swept along a bare half-inch above the dirt of the yard. I knew she couldn't be used to such shoes and hemlines, yet she picked her way through the junk of the yard as unerringly as a goat on a mountain.

Where she got the dress I still don't know. Either there is a tall girls' wedding shop somewhere or a brilliant seamstress with an enormous sewing table. I have seen a lot of wedding dresses, but Bernice's was the most beautiful of them all—the whitest, the laciest, the best designed dress I have ever seen.

Her face was still the same—totally devoid of makeup. Her hair had not changed—still completely without body or life. But her eyes! They glistened and blazed and bannered forth the message: "World, I am getting married! I am the tall-girl bride." I did not know whether the dress had changed her or she had enchanted the dress. I did know that she was in charge.

She ushered me between a stack of old tires and a pile of broken bricks into a scene from Danté.

The front room was the size of the smallest of the four bedrooms in my parsonage home. At least 30 people had been sweat-fitted into it. Each was smoking a cigar or cigarette. The ceiling was about six inches above my head, and the whole top half of the room looked like Mount St. Helens had just erupted. The tiara-like clasp of Bernice's veil had to be scraping the pressed board above, but I was not sure because I could not tell where its white gauze ended and the smoke began. An oil burner stood a few feet from the wall at one end of the room. I couldn't see its thermostat, but I didn't need to. I knew it was turned to ultra-high.

Half the people in the room displayed the high cheekbones and lank hair of Appalachia. The other half flashed the black eyes and brown skin of Mexico. Between puffs, every person in the room was speaking a language or accent foreign to me. I felt like some early missionary, being presented to the tribal elders by the queen.

She took me by the hand and pulled me into a second room, bending almost in half as she led me through the door. The ceiling here was no more than five feet above the uncarpeted floor. I got only a quick glance at the room, being concerned for my own head, but there were three or four beds; that was all.

We squeezed through one more door and came abruptly to the end of the house. This was the kitchen, with enough headroom to stand in. She pointed with pride at the single-layer cake she had baked herself. One end was two inches higher than the other.

Then she shooed the entire kitchen crew into the front room.

I was placed at the end away from the oil burner, my back to the rough-framed, square window that covered almost the entire end wall.

They stood before me, Roland in a brown and green plaid polyester sportcoat and wrinkled black trousers. The best man slouched behind him, looking exactly like the "gunsel" in *Maltese Falcon*, smoking a cigarette. There was no room for the maid of honor to stand, so she sat on the lap of the man who was in the only chair at that end of the room. He put his arm around her, just under her bosom. Throughout the ceremony he kept pushing one or the other of her breasts up out of her low-cut dress. I immediately thought of pop-tarts. Each time she popped, everyone on the other side of the room roared their approval, as the maid of honor herself giggled and pushed herself back down into her dress.

I raised my eyes from my service book, focused steadily on the bride and groom, resisted the urge to look down when I heard giggles, and discovered to my amazement that I knew the service by heart.

No one stopped smoking. No one stopped talking. Bernice and Roland concentrated hard to hear what I said.

Just after they exchanged rings, Uncle *Rex arrived. He weighed at least 300 pounds and was smoking a cigar that looked like his twin brother. He had also been drinking for a while—about four days would be my guess. There was no space in the room for Uncle Rex, but he came in anyway, like the granddaddy shark at feeding-frenzy time. He seized Bernice, plucked out his cigar, and pulled her down to his height for a wheezy kiss. The lighted end of his cigar charred a big, ugly, brown hole in her veil. Bernice assured Uncle Rex it was alright, although he had not apologized.

Uncle Rex then assured me it was okay for me to carry on now that he was there. I carried on, but by this time I was sure the stress had been too much for Bernice. She kept winking over my shoulder. Once she stuck her tongue out and grinned.

I pronounced them, prayed over them, blessed them, gave Bernice a peck on the cheek, and escaped through the giggles and the smoke to the quiet relief of the inanimate junk in the front yard.

As I slipped into the blessed middle-classness of my station wagon, I saw why Bernice had been winking and sticking her tongue out. Every urchin in the neighborhood was peering through the window that had been behind me, watching the show.

Irish 80 is a dead-end neighborhood in every way. I tried to leave by the quickest route, the way my car was already pointed, but I was consistently turned back by railroad levees and factory buildings.

The only way out was the way I came in.

So I drove back by Bernice's house again. She did not see me. I was glad; it would have broken the spell. She stood in the yard, before the handpainted car with the colors that looked like they came right out of a crayon box, the big pack, in a circle of children, pointing out the various features of her dress, executing a flowing turn so they could watch the train swirl around her. In my rearview mirror I saw her smile as she stuck her finger through the hole in the veil made by Uncle Rex's cigar.

She was the prettiest tall-girl bride ever, and I'm the man you come to when there's no place else to go.

la(s)t rites

I was in the psych ward, so I was wearing a clerical collar.
Light blue shirt, to be sure no one thought I took the collar,
or myself, too seriously. But the collar provides instant identification and credibility. It gets you through various doors
with a minimum of hassle, especially in the psych ward.

It can also get you into trouble.

The announcement came through the speaker overhead.

"Any minister in the building. Any minister in the building. Please report to the third-floor nurses' station."

I heard it, heard what it said, but I didn't pay attention to
it. I was deeply into conversation with *Gladys, one of my
members. I didn't know her well. I hadn't been pastor there
long. She hadn't come to church much. If she were in the
psych ward, though, I knew not to break off a conversation
just because of a public announcement. Besides, I knew they
didn't want *all* the ministers in the building. There were
bound to be others.

The announcement was repeated. I kept listening to
Gladys. A flustered nurse showed up at my elbow.

"Uh, I'm sorry to interrupt, but . . . there's a lady dying
down on three, and they've looked all over the building for a
minister and can't find one, and I, uh, well, I noticed your
collar . . ."

"Go ahead," said Gladys. "I've had my problems a long
time. They'll still be here when you get back."

I hurried down to the third-floor nurse's station.

"This lady's Catholic," they told me, "and we've tried
every priest within 30 miles and can't find any of them, so
we thought we'd better just put out a broadside for anyone."

I was, apparently, the only "anyone" available.

I went to the Catholic lady's room. She looked at my
collar and seemed relieved.

"I'm sorry, but in spite of the collar, I'm not a priest," I warned her. "I'm a United Methodist pastor. The nurses asked me to come in to see you. I can read Scripture and pray with you. I also know how to give the last rites of your church, so if you'd like, I'll do that for you, even though I'm not a priest, and even though I don't have the special things a priest uses for that ritual."

She sighed and nodded, a nod that said, "Well, it's better than nothing."

I scriptured. I prayed. I started the last rites. I had studied the Roman Catholic rituals in seminary 25 years before, when this one was still called "extreme unction." I quickly found myself in extreme difficulty. I didn't remember nearly as much of the ritual as I thought I would. But, what the heck, it wasn't the real thing anyway. I filled in with whatever seemed reasonable, including some Latin, some Greek, some Hebrew, some French. It was going great.

Then the housekeeper came in, with bucket and mop. I was standing beside the bed of a woman on death's door, wearing a clerical collar, mumbling "*Kyrie eleison*," and she started mopping. She mopped all around the bed until she came to me.

"Lift your left foot," she said.

"*And by the power of the Holy Spirit . . .*," I intoned as I lifted my left foot. She mopped where my left foot had been.

"Lift your right foot," she said.

It is said that angels can fly because they take themselves so lightly. I did not take myself that lightly, so I put my left down before raising my right.

"*. . . through the love of our Savior . . .*"

She mopped where my right foot had been.

The lady in the bed raised her eyebrows. I shrugged my shoulders. The housekeeper left. In the doorway she collided with an empty wheelchair driven by a white-coated woman from the x-ray department. The mop bucket turned over.

Dirty water flowed, and dirty words, words of recrimination and disdain.

"*. . . that the Lord may take us unto himself . . .*"

The mop lady started all over.

"Lift your left foot," she said.

"*. . . that where he is, we may be also . . .*"

We repeated the ritual of the mop bucket.

The wheelchair lady went behind the curtain to the woman in the next bed.

"I've come to get you for your x-ray, Mabel," she announced. She had once been a conductor in the Chicago subway system.

"*. . . because we know not what a day may bring forth . . .*"

Mabel had once been a sailor. She had approximately the same use for women from x-ray that she had for diseased parrots. She suggested, loudly, what the x-ray lady could do with her wheelchair. It sounded rather painful.

"I'm not going to take any excrement from you today," the x-ray lady told her, not exactly in those words.

"Raise your right foot."

"*. . . but that the hour for serving Thee is always present. . .*"

Good grief, I had gone off into the funeral ritual!

"Get that less-than-admirable wheelchair away from me," being a loose translation of Mabel.

The sun was coming through the window to the far side of the x-ray lady and Mabel. It provided a shadow show through the curtain, as the x-ray lady climbed onto the bed and began to extract Mabel.

"You get various parts of your slender anatomy out of that bed and into this chair," being a loose translation from the x-ray lady.

"*. . . let us awake to the instant claims . . .*"

"Idiots," said the mop lady as she left.

A struggle ensued in the next bed. After a few more phrases from me, the lady from x-ray emerged, her white jacket hanging off one shoulder, her hair looking for all the world like Medusa, but triumphantly pushing a scowling and still voluble Mabel in the wheelchair.

"... *of thy holy will* ..."

The lady in the bed began to giggle. So did I. I took her hand. We laughed. We cried. It may have been the best praying I ever did with a patient.

I saw her obituary in the newspaper six months later.

the will of God

The telephone rang, but I didn't even bother to walk down the hall from my upstairs study. Helen was beside a phone in the kitchen. Our daughters were teenagers; nine out of 10 calls were for them. In the unlikely event it was for me, they'd probably talk for 10 minutes first just out of habit. I could afford to wait and see.

Then, however, I heard them crying, all of them, Helen and Mary Beth and Katie, not the usual tears that are a part of living in a house full of women, but sobbing, screaming, then heavy footsteps pounding on the steps as they ran upstairs to find me. This time I couldn't afford to wait and see. I was up out of my chair and running down the hall. We met at the top of the stairs.

"It's Mary V.," Helen gasped out between her heaves. "Steve and Tony were just killed in a car wreck."

The girls huddled behind her, as though she were a shield, holding onto each other as they so often have when there was need to weep.

I went to the phone like a zombie, to hear from my sister's own lips the story of the death of her babies, the youngest of her five sons, 18 and 19 years old. My older sister, my anchor in childhood storms, for whom I had traded my life, was telling me that two wondrously bright young lives had been snuffed out, and there was nothing we could do about it. I had nothing now to trade for the lives of her children, nor did she. It was too late.

"Two other boys were killed with them," she said. "They were longtime friends. They've been in and out of our house since they were little kids. I feel like I've lost four sons instead of two."

Mary V. was calm. She's always calm, but the wilder the storms blow around her, the stiller she stands. She would do her own telephoning to give bad news. She would do her own weeping in private.

"I'm coming on the first plane," I told her.

There wasn't anything I could do. I just had to be there.

I didn't know how long I'd be there; I hadn't even asked about when memorial services would be. Illinois to California is an expensive trip. The girls were in school. Helen needed to be with them if I couldn't be. For a lot of reasons, I went alone. I didn't want to go alone, didn't want to sit on a plane full of people who drank canned orange juice and ate plastic chicken without having the slightest idea of the emptiness I felt. But I went.

As I flew through the air, surrounded by innocently ignorant strangers, I thought about Steve and Tony, such sweet boys, such delightful young men. Tall, slender Steve, with a thousand friends—the actor, the entertainer, even when he wasn't on stage. Handsome, curly-headed Tony, "Uncle Brillo" the other boys called him—the quarterback, college-bound on an athletic scholarship.

John Howard, the oldest son, picked me up at L.A.X.

"We'd all been in the mountains, skiing," he told me. "Tony was driving the first car. I was driving the second. We didn't leave together. They went first. We weren't ready. If they'd just waited for us, then they wouldn't have been at that spot in the road when the truck came over the hill."

I knew what Mary V. would say to that. When we got there, she did.

"There's no point in playing 'what if,' " she said to John Howard. "It happened. Now we deal with it."

She turned to the other John in her kitchen, John Robert, her brother, the preacher.

"We want you to do the service."

I didn't want to do the service. I didn't feel like a preacher. I felt like a mourner, an uncle, a brother, someone who had nothing to say, who could only listen. I didn't know if I *could* do the service. What if I broke down crying in the middle of it? What good would that do anyone? But this was too important to be left to amateurs, or to strangers. There wasn't anyone else who could do that service the way I could. I was family, and I was called. It was a gift I could give to my sister, that I could give to my brother-in-law, Dick, to John Howard and Mike and Jeff and all the others who loved Steve and Tony. I didn't want to do it, but I did.

There were four services. There was a community service at the Lutheran church for all four boys. I spoke at that, along with the pastors of the other boys. There were individual services later that day for the two boys who were killed with Steve and Tony. Finally, the next day, there would be the service for my nephews.

That night, though, the brother of one of the other boys who had been killed was in an accident. He was driving, speeding, carelessly racing through the town. His car was a mess, but he got away with cuts and bruises.

"How could you do this?" I asked. "Your brother lies cold in the ground. You're all your parents have left. How could you go out and drive like a madman the very night after your brother was buried?"

"Nothing I can do about it," he said. "When it happens, it happens. If your time comes, that's it."

It's a wonderfully guilt-free way to wander though life, isn't it? Fatalism is so appealing. It takes all responsibility from us. The speed at which I drive, the rate at which I smoke, the carelessness with which I eat—none of it has anything to do with my outcome. What I do this moment is not connected with the next. I am not responsible for my life or for my death or for the suffering of those who love me.

There's a religious fatalism. It's called "the will of God." We use it at the time of death. Regardless of the circumstances of the death, or its gruesomeness, or its enormity, there will always be someone who says, "Well, it was the will of God." I hadn't used quite those words, but that was what I had said to the family of Billy Quick, back there in Chrisney, all those years ago.

The funeral home was large, as large as most church sanctuaries, but it couldn't begin to hold the crowd. The funeral directors were prepared. They had set up loud speakers on their lawn and in their parking lot. Hundreds of people parked their cars for blocks around and walked to the funeral home and stood in the California sun and surrounded us with their caring.

It comes over me at those times, when death sits on two closed, smooth, wood coffins at the foot of the pulpit, when there's nothing that can be said and yet that nothing must be spoken.

I'm always prepared. I've thought and prayed it through. I use no notes, no manuscript, but I know what I will say. I say it. Yet they are not my words, even though it was my brain that thought them, and it is my voice that speaks them. Somehow I'm pulled up beyond what I have prepared. Words that would otherwise be mere balloons above my head, as in a cartoon, take on meaning that I could not give them.

I speak no easy grace at the time of death. Platitudes hold no comfort. I try to speak the truth, as unvarnished as a plain wood coffin, the truth of how speed and carelessness kill, the truth that God's will is thwarted when young lives are pulled from the face of the earth in a mass of mangled man-made steel. There is deep comfort in the truth, the truth that such is *not* the will of God.

"Blessed are those who mourn, for they shall be comforted." Good grief, real mourning, comes only when we understand that the will of God is thwarted every time violence on earth comes like a thief and snatches away one of God's children. I said it over, and over, and over again: "This was *not* the will of God!"

That night, after the service, after supper, Dick and I sat together in his den, smoking our pipes. One of his friends came by. He sat with us for a while and talked uneasily of trivial things. Finally, he said to me . . .

"Well, as you said this afternoon, it was the will of God."

My pipe almost fell from my mouth. Where had this man been? I had spent half my time that afternoon helping people understand that these deaths were *not* the will of God!

Then it came over me again, settled down like a flannel blanket on a cold night, and I understood.

He had heard. He knew the truth. He knew that God had no timetable, that God had not reached down and thrown Tony's car in front of a truck. He wasn't trying to escape responsibility, like the fatalistic brother. That's not what he meant by "the will of God." He was just trying to say, with the only phrase he knew for it, that God is still in charge, that God will create something out of chaos, that death is not the end of God's plan for young lives, or even for old ones.

"Yes," I said. "It was the will of God."

"but did you have @ good time?"

The only problem, as I saw it, was that I would miss Katie's graduation from Indiana University. I really wanted to see Katie graduate. I had been there for Mary Beth's commencement, so proud of my bright and beautiful daughter. Now it was Katie's turn, and she was my last child, and thus my last chance. How often, though, do you get a chance to visit missionaries in a war zone?

I'd been invited to go to Nicaragua, in the company of about 15 others from our annual conference, to visit Howard and Peggy Heiner, United Methodists, a forester and a nurse, respectively. We were to carry in about 18 donated sewing machines for a widows' sewing cooperative, plus medicines. We would travel around the country, seeing firsthand the work of missionaries in a land that was the symbol of U.S. resistance to Communism, especially Castroism, in the Western Hemisphere.

It was 1986. The Sandinistas were in power, having overthrown the U.S.-supported Somoza dictatorship in 1979. They were named for a famous guerrilla fighter, Augusto Sandino, who had fought the U.S. Marines when they had occupied Nicaragua as a protectorate, from 1911 to 1933. The Sandinistas had fought a long civil war to depose Somoza, but the war was not over. Remnants of Somoza's National Guard, supported by the U.S., had gone into the hills and had themselves become a guerrilla force, fighting the new government. They were called the Contras. We would be in the capital city of Managua, where the war rarely reached, except in the suffering of families who lost soldiers in the hills, but we would also be in provincial cities such as Esteli' and in smaller towns and open country where the war was a daily reality.

I was convinced the U.S. was wrong about Nicaragua, that we had been wrong to support the brutal Somoza, and that we were wrong to support the Contras. I believed there had been too much killing and that it was time for reconciliation. I hoped the church could play a role in bringing peace. If that were possible, I wanted to help it happen. I wanted to see Nicaragua firsthand, talk to people on both sides, learn what could be done to insure both peace and freedom.

So I went. But I had to miss Katie's graduation.

In the summer following her first year in college, Katie had been working at the dining table one night, figuring out her class schedule for the coming year. I was trying to read in the living room, but Katie was as distracting as a bedroom mosquito, muttering imprecations and breaking pencils.

"What's wrong?" I asked.

"I can't get my classes arranged so they won't interfere with my social life," she wailed.

That is a really bad line to use on a man who is paying out-of-state tuition.

"Social life? What do you think you are in college for, anyway? You act like you think the point of life is to have a good time!"

"Well, isn't it?" she asked, eyes wide with fake innocence.

"Of course not," I bellowed. "Where did you ever get an idea like that?"

"Why, from listening to your preaching."

Now that was almost too much. *My* preaching? "Reverend Commitment's" preaching? She had to be kidding! I had always been a good, responsible person. I worked hard. I did the right things in the right ways. I was called to the ministry, for God's sake, not to happiness. I was called to take up my cross daily, to suffer, not to have a good time. If any good times slipped in, it certainly wasn't my fault!

I had 2,000 years of Christian history backing me up. I knew it was not a typo when the School of Theology in

Claremont, California, printed in its commencement program the response of its graduates as, "We commit sourselves to ministry."

I heard about a boy who visited his grandmother on the farm one Sunday. Bored, he tried to find something to do. Play ball? Read comic books? Mow the grass, even? "No, you can't do that on the Sabbath," she kept telling him. He finally wandered down to the barnyard and there saw a mule leaning his long, sad head down over the fence. "Poor fellow," he said. "You must be a Christian, too."

Well, of course. That's the ideal Christian, isn't it?

Katie's reply, however, started me thinking. I even began to pay attention to my own preaching. Now, any preacher can tell you that is a dangerous thing to do. Look at what happened to Billy Graham when he started listening to his own preaching. He became a peacenik and lost a lot of friends. The problem was, Katie was right. I'd been preaching the gospel, but I hadn't been listening to it.

What amazes me now is that it took me so long to understand that the point of life really *is* to have a good time. After all, I've been both an American and a Christian all my life. What's the American creed? "Life, Liberty, and the Pursuit of Happiness." The pursuit of responsibility? The pursuit of productivity? The pursuit of truth? No, the pursuit of *happiness*! What did Jesus say? "Let the good times roll."[1]

Of course, he was accused of being a winebibber and a glutton. I suspect that was not because he was those things, but because the good people of his time—the responsible people, the people who wouldn't let their social lives interfere with their class schedules—thought that any good time at all was too much, especially for one who claimed to come from God.

The problem is this: What is a good time? The biggest stumbling block on the road to a truly good time is a false good time, and there are plenty of those garishly displayed on the smorgasbord of life.

I've never had much trouble recognizing the false good times for what they are. It was several years later, though, after Katie's struggle with her class schedule, through the loss of a good deal of my guts, before I understood, down in what was left of my guts, that what each of us is really called to in this life is a good time, a time that doesn't allow our responsibility schedule to interfere with our relationship schedule, that doesn't let works become a stumbling block to grace.

So there I was in Nicaragua, missing the graduation of my daughter, who had set me on the road to a good time, although for me, it was still a principle of how one ought to live more than a reality of how I did live.

One day we were in the mountains, out several hours from Esteli'. We didn't really know where we were. We had been guided back into the fighting zone by a Sandinista officer, to a front-line camp, no more than a mile from where Sandinista and Contra patrols engaged in fire fights.

One patrol came back to camp while we were there. It was composed of 14 and 15 year-old-boys, with a 19-year-old officer, the "old man." Carrying their smoking rifles, they were running up and down the ditches, back and forth across the roads, grabbing one another's hats, throwing them to someone else, chasing and being chased, whooping and laughing. Just boys, having a good time, not letting their schedule of fighting interrupt their social life.

When they saw Marisol, our tour guide, a voluptuous and beautiful young woman in her early 20s, they crowded around her in trance-like concentration, not wanting to miss even the slightest movement of this magnificent creature. The officer quickly offered to show Marisol how to fire a rifle, and, of course, had to put his arms around her to demonstrate proper technique. The boys cheered and clapped each time she fired a round, not even being too careful about where they were standing when she fired. When we had to leave, they didn't seem so much disappointed by her departure as thankful that they had experienced even a few moments in the radiance of the marvelous Marisol. Just boys, having a good time, not letting their schedule of killing disrupt their social lives.

When we got back to Managua, it was Katie's graduation day. I had done the best I could to make up for my absence. Katie was a fanatic supporter of IU's soccer team, consistent Big 10 and NCAA champions. I had arranged, secretly, to get a special gift for her graduation present—a soccer ball that the team had used in one of its wins. Knowing the circumstances, the team did me proud. They didn't just send the ball; they all signed it, and on graduation day, delivered it.

I telephoned Katie at her dorm room just before she had to leave for Assembly Hall for graduation exercises. She thanked me for the ball, but it wasn't what was on my mind.

"Well, how do you feel about your education?" I asked.

"It must have been okay," she replied. "I get to wear a gold cord because I'm an honors graduate of the honors division. I made Phi Beta Kappa. I'm a Rhodes Scholar nominee."

I knew all that, but it worried me to hear her say it. It sounded too much like she'd allowed her class schedule to interfere with her social life.

"But . . . I guess what I really want to know," I stammered, "is . . . did you have a good time?"

There was a long pause, and I could hear her wonderment all the way from Bloomington, Indiana, to Managua, Nicaragua. Then she said,

"Of course I had a good time. I *am* a Christian, you know."

note

[1]John 10:10b. This passage is usually mistranslated as "I came that they may have life, and have it abundantly." It means the same thing.

bapti(z)ing Charles

I should never have been talking with the murderer in the county jail anyway. They said he had sent for me, but that was a mistake. I didn't know that then, though. He had told the jail ministry volunteers that he wanted to talk to the pastor of the Wesleyan Church on Fourth Street. I pastored Wesley Church (United Methodist) on South Fourth Street. Since most of the volunteers were members of my congregation, they naturally heard Wesley instead of Wesleyan.

"Charles wants to talk to you about getting baptized," they said. "You'd better go down to the jail and see him."

I didn't want to talk with Charles. I didn't know him. We could find no trace of him in any of our records. He was accused of killing his wife, a former high school student of my wife's. I didn't know if he'd done it, but I didn't know what to say to him either way. I didn't want to go to see Charles in the county jail, so I did what pastors always do when they don't want to do some part of their job. I went. If you're called, you're supposed to go.

He was lean and sunken-eyed and long-haired, shrouded in an orange jumpsuit much too large for him. We sat on opposite sides of a thick, smeared glass and talked to each other through the little holes like they have in movie theaters so you can't kiss the ticket seller. I felt like saying, "Two tickets for Bird Man of Alcatraz, please."

Over a period of weeks, this is what Charles told me:

"Everything was going so well. I was getting good grades at the junior college. She was pregnant with my baby. We were happy. Then she started messing around with this other guy while I was at school, even with the baby inside her. I didn't mean to kill her. We were sitting beside each other on the bed. She started telling me all about it. I just put my arm around her neck to keep her from saying those awful things. When she stopped talking, I took my arm away. She was dead. My arm had just shut off all her wind.[1] I want to be baptized so I can commit suicide. I'm probably going to jail for the rest of my life. Right now I'm at peace with God. But I'm a weak man. If I go to prison, I'll end up being a bad man. I'll do things there that I'll get sent to hell for. I'm not going to be any good to anyone here. I've messed up this life. Baptize me so I can get on to the next one."[2]

I couldn't baptize Charles so he could commit suicide. Knowing his intention, it was probably illegal and at least unethical. But did I have a right to withhold from a prisoner a rite of the church?

I tried to explain that baptism is not an automatic ticket to heaven, or that dying without it means one will go to hell.[3] That was beside the point. Charles had an exceptionally good argument. Didn't it make sense for him to get out of this life before he did anything else that would send him straight to hell? That made sense to me, whether hell is something here and now or something then and there.

We continued our talks. I finally agreed to baptize him, but not so he could commit suicide. In fact, I guaranteed him that he would go straight to hell for sure if he committed suicide after baptism, even though I had no authority in heaven or on earth to make such a guarantee. I would baptize him only for the usual reason, as the first step into Christian life. Charles was a weak man; he agreed.

Baptism is an act of confirmation rather than of creation. It doesn't cause God to start caring for or loving a person. That care and love is already there. Baptism acknowledges it. Also, baptism is a rite of the church, not just of the pastor. It is the first step into church membership, not just into a private relationship with God. Normally, thus, we perform the ritual only in the presence of the congregation, which almost always means in a worship service. There was no way Charles could get out of jail to go to church, so I took the church to him, in the presence of the Lay Leader of the congregation, Lee Steinmetz, a professor of English, a scholar of Latin, a reader of science fiction and Western novels, a writer of books, a singer of solos in the church choir. Lee is tall and bearded and a little flaky. I like him. He reminds me of me.

We took to the jail the liner of the baptismal font from church, so that Charles would be baptized from the same bowl as everyone else. They put us in the "library," a room about four-feet square, with one chair, a wire rack, and one old *Reader's Digest.* I asked the deputy to bring me some water in the baptismal bowl. He did. Apparently he was a Baptist and thought I wanted to immerse Charles. He had filled it to the brim. Above the brim, even, the way water sometimes does when the molecules adhere so closely that they just keep on going up, rim or no rim, the way "Dr. J"[4] used to hang in the air above the rim with no visible means of support.

The deputy seemed disappointed when, after I had baptized Charles by dripping a little water on his head from my hands, he had to go back down the hall and pour out about four gallons of extra water. Perhaps I should have just gone up and down the halls and kept on baptizing until it was gone.

I sat through Charles' trial. His lawyer pleaded him innocent. No one but me knew at that time the story of how he had actually killed his wife. The prosecutor hadn't heard it from Charles, but she had figured it out. One of my church members was on his jury. I tried not to look at her, for fear she could read my face. I hoped, however, that they would find him guilty, for I knew he was guilty. I also hoped they wouldn't send him to prison, for I knew he was weak.

They convicted him. He got 15 years. I knew it was too long for a weak man like Charles. He was out in seven and a half. It was still too long.

We had moved away, so I didn't know he was out until I caught his name on the television news. The baptism hadn't changed him much, nor had prison. He had raped and beaten and mutilated his new girlfriend. He claimed it was under the influence of drugs. He went to prison again. He won't get out this time. This time he committed suicide.

Charles knew himself well. He knew he was too weak, that he needed some supernatural strength to overcome his weakness. I think that strength exists, but you don't lay hold of it just through the water of baptism.

There ought to be a place for weak men like Charles, a place where they can go and be protected from themselves, while others also are protected from them, but if it exists, it's not in this life.

Maybe it would have been better for everyone if I had just baptized Charles and let him commit suicide. Perhaps he was too weak even for that.

I've learned not to feel guilty over things I can't control. We pastors do the best we can, with the resources at hand, but we can't run other people's lives, nor should we. I didn't make Charles weak. I had no way of pulling his arm away from his wife's neck, no way of hiding his hammer before he beat his girlfriend with it. On the other hand, even though I had the water of baptism at my command, I couldn't make him strong either.

notes

[1] This was consistent with the pathological report.

[2] Some of what I knew I had learned in confidence, but it all became part of the public record from sources other than myself as time passed.

[3] Some churches disagree with this point.

[4] Julius Erving, retired professional basketball player.

Barbara'Ⓢ murder

It was a Tuesday. Eight in the evening. Late September. It felt more like late November. I walked the mile to *Carla's house, pre-winter wind at my back, dusty half-moon above my head, stone in my stomach.

I was just getting settled on a straight chair in the family room, under the awkward gaze of the committee members, when the phone rang. Carla stepped into the kitchen to answer it. She came back immediately and beckoned to me. She led me into *Don's den so I could take the call there.

I was relieved. This was a meeting of the Pastor-Parish Relations Committee to discuss my salary for the coming year. The committee had been at Carla's house for an hour already, planning how they could plead poverty and explain why they couldn't give me a raise again. It happened every year. I was used to it, just an annual insult. I wasn't looking forward to it. It made me ashamed. I don't like being ashamed of my own church members.

I was so pleased at postponing my date with the debtors that I didn't stop to think of who might be on the phone.

It was *Rick Lyons. Funeral Director Rick Lyons. That was okay. Good funeral directors call the minister first, which means they call at any hour. Our church had a thousand members. There was always someone ready to die. The funeral directors called me often.

I had forgotten that Rick Lyons was also the coroner.

He didn't bother to explain how he knew where I was.

"I'll be by to get you in about two minutes," he said, his voice tense. "*Barbara Tenhove's been murdered. I don't have many details, except that her boyfriend did it. We've got to get over to her parents' house before some nut picks it up on a police scanner and telephones them. Stand on the west side of the street so I can keep going south. It'll be faster to loop around the university that way."

I stepped into the hallway and back to the family room. The faces on the committee members, which had seemed so grim a moment before, now looked warm and beckoning. I longed to spend the evening with these good people, these alive people, listening happily to why they couldn't give me a raise, instead of doing what I had to do.

I motioned Carla over.

"I have to leave," I whispered. "I'm sure I won't be back tonight, so go ahead with your business. I can't explain why right now, but . . . well, pray for me, please, and pray for those I'm going to see."

I grabbed my coat and went out to stand on the west side of the street, standing in a late September wind that stabbed now to the bone, waiting for Rick, hoping it was all a mistake. But I knew it wasn't. Nothing ever went right for Barbara, and no one ever knew why.

She was 23 years old. Pretty and lively. Friend of my daughters. In some ways like another daughter to me. We had spent so much time together, counseling, encouraging, wrestling with her demons. A late-life baby with three older sisters. Her parents were good people, two of our best members, and my faithful supporters.

In the slant pre-winter wind I stood, wrestling now with my own demons, wanting to wreak havoc on her boyfriend . . . wanting to put my arms around *Norman and *Laura and Barbara's sisters, and knowing it would do no good . . . wanting to pull Barbara back from the grave so I could give her a good spanking for insisting on going out with that terrible loser of a poor boy, when we'd all warned her against it . . . wanting to avoid wondering if our warnings were what made her do it . . . wanting just to walk down the street and turn west, into the wind, and go home . . . wanting to sneak a glance at the dusty moon and insisting to know why these things were allowed to happen . . . and Rick pulled up in his black Chevy.

I have no idea how long I was at the house or what time I got home. We sat together, cried together, wondered together, forgave together. We made a hundred phone calls. Neighbors came and went. In the middle of the night people showed up with jugs of coffee and chocolate cakes. So we ate together, too—wine in white mugs, bread dark on our forks, remembering other meals, hoping for an eternal banquet. Each of us with all the others, each of us with Barbara, each of us alone.

Barbara's psychiatrist came. Outside his office he looked so small, so lost, like a general whose war had run off. We both had treated Barbara, he with medicine and Freud of Vienna's "talking cure," me with prayers and Jesus of Nazareth's listening cure, with equal lack of success. It was the first time, however, we had met.

He beckoned me into a corner behind an artificial ficus tree, a plate of cake below his chin, tears upon his cheeks. He asked me why it had happened. He asked me what else he could have done. He asked me how her parents were going to cope. He asked me what he should do now.

Pastors don't have answers, although some of us act like we do, because we think we should. Good pastors simply stand with people, and kneel with them, as they ask the questions. I have known many psychiatrists, but he is the only one I ever pastored. He is the only one who ever asked the questions.

After midnight *Sheila decided she needed to go to the morgue at the hospital to see her sister. Some people need to see. Others don't. No one else wanted to go. I got behind the wheel of Sheila's little car and drove her out into the country, out to the new hospital, standing stark against the prairie, under the dusty moon.

The deputy didn't much want us to go into the basement room where Barbara lay in a hospital bed, as though she had simply been a patient. He seemed to expect some sort of hysterical scene. He warned us against touching "the body," since it would be sent to the crime lab at the state capital. He started to go in with us, but I warned him off with a glare and a toss of my head. This was private time.

We stood at a distance, staring at her, then moved up closer. We didn't touch her, but not because of the deputy. We could touch her better by holding each other, which we did. We could speak to her best with our tears. We did that, too.

The funeral was at the church building. There were many people I had never seen inside those walls before, including the psychiatrist. We sang and prayed. I spoke of Barbara, and of the people who loved her, and of the boy who killed her. I spoke of memories and love and hope and forgiveness. I spoke of the God who has enough hands to hold all of us up, even though we cannot see any of those hands, even though we can feel only the one that surrounds us.

It's not a very efficient way for a powerful and divine God to work out that hands business, but it's the one we're stuck with, it seems. I said that, too. Barbara's parents and sisters laughed. The psychiatrist looked like a man who wanted to, but didn't know why.

The family asked for permission to bury Barbara's ashes under a tree on the church lawn. The trustees turned them down. Didn't want to set a precedent, they said. So the family asked for permission to plant a tree in her memory. The trustees turned that down, too. They didn't know where the new sanctuary would be built, they said, and they didn't want to have to dig up any trees that were in the way when they got around to building it.

In the spring on a well-known holiday when no one else was at the church building, Barbara's family and I brought a little tree to a hidden corner on the lee side of the building between the chapel and my office. We dug a hole and poured in Barbara's ashes and planted the tree above them.

Ten years later the new sanctuary was built. The tree was removed. No one knew about Barbara's ashes. They're under the new pulpit.

I didn't know what happened at the committee meeting until I got my first paycheck in January.

"there is no ⓢtory that is not true."

I once preached to a gathering of some 12 or 13 hundred souls, half of them ministers, half laity. Afterward I heard a prestigious, very conservative minister telling some of his friends how much he appreciated my sermon. I was a bit surprised by this because we have very little in common, except that we appreciate each other's commitment. "Oh, he's just a storyteller," one of them replied.

He was, of course, right.

That's how I started, telling stories, and that's what I've been doing ever since, when I was supposed to be preaching. At the age of 19 I didn't know how to preach, but I knew how to tell a story. I grew up with stories. Stories were what I remembered from the sermons I had heard at Forsythe Church. Stories were what I remembered.

I'm sure that Paul Burns and Kenwood Bryant and Gene Matthews, the lay preachers who came to Forsythe on Sunday mornings to "fill the pulpit," did "real" preaching, not "just storytelling." They were, however, without formal education in ministry. Paul was a postmaster; Ken, a school-teacher; Gene, a factory worker. Their sermons were not sophisticated theologically. They just tried to remind us that God loves us and that we should do the best we can to be part of the solution instead of part of the problem. They did it best with stories—the great narratives of the Bible, homely little anecdotes from their family lives or work experiences, retellings from that great treasure chest of "preacher stories" that circulate from one preacher to another.[1] That was what we remembered from their sermons, what we went home and told others—the stories. If anyone had said to us, "But what was the 'point' of the sermon?" we'd have been unable to answer, except to say, "Well, he told about the little boy who fell out of bed and said it was because he went to sleep too close to where he got in." We didn't remember the "real" preaching; we remembered the stories.

When I was in seminary, I was considerably embarrassed in preaching class because the other students preached reams of closely reasoned theology, explaining studiously how Kierkegaard and Schliermacher differed on soteriology and what this meant for our salvation. I told about the man who offered the $10,000 reward for the return of his wife's pet cat. His friends were amazed at such generosity because he hated that cat. He knew, however, that he had already drowned and buried the cat. "When you know what you know," he said, "you can afford to be extravagant." They were preachers; I was "just a storyteller."

But each week, when we all returned to classes after our Sunday preaching, they complained that their charges never remembered their well-reasoned and orderly exposition of the 11th chapter of Hebrews over against the writings of Irenaeus.

"They never remember the points of my sermon," they lamented. "All they remember are the illustrations."

By illustrations, of course, they meant the stories. I was not bold enough to say it out loud, but I began to think it: If that's what they remember, maybe the illustrations are the points, and the points are the illustrations. Maybe it's the story that is the real preaching, and the other stuff we say is context so we can enjoy the story more.

Later I learned to speak of narrative as first-level language, the level at which we actually live, and exposition and proposition as second-level language, the abstract level we use to talk *about* the actual living. Just what I'm doing now —writing in second-level language about first-level language. Second level is good and helpful. We couldn't get along without it. One of the constant dangers of preaching, though, is to confuse the two, to get them upside down, to think and talk and preach as if the abstractions are life and life is just an "illustration" of what we *think* about it.

I think the greatest danger of preaching is being boring, especially to oneself. As a preacher, you are not supposed to preach new ideas. You are supposed to be faithful to the revelation of God, not create a new faith. You need to have new ways to express those old ideas, though, ways that will cause your listeners to say "Aha!" instead of "Ho-hum." I think my greatest fear as a preacher has always been that I would be a deadhead, boring. I don't mean boring in the sense of not entertaining. In truth, there are preachers who are entertaining, but that's all they are. A preacher doesn't need to be entertaining to escape boredom. She or he just needs to stay with the story.

Boredom almost always slips in unnoticed on the dreary coattails of second-level language. See, aren't you a little bored right now? My point, exactly. You're starting to say to yourself, "When is he going to get back to the story?" It's just like listening to a sermon, isn't it?

When Bishop Fulton Sheen was at the height of his pulpit popularity, he was asked if it didn't get boring, since he had to preach so often, and thus had to preach the same sermon over and over. "Well, I preach the same sermon," he said, "but with different gestures."

Somehow preachers manage to make the greatest story in the world boring, and it's because we forget it's a story. We talk about the story instead of telling it. God's not a theologian. God's just a storyteller.

Narrative preaching is dangerous, so it's not surprising that we shy away from it. It invites people to live in the story, to be in the story, to exist at the point where God's story and their story intersect. It calls for action and change. Preachers aren't all that comfortable with action and change, in part because we were taught by teachers to be teachers.

There's a vast difference between teaching and preaching. Someone once described a preacher by saying, "His preaching was hot truth let loose." You're not likely to hear that said about a teacher, unless she or he has "gone to preaching." I don't mean to denigrate teaching. It's an important and honorable activity. Pastors do teach, as well as preach. We preach, though, not to impart information or to inculcate wisdom. We preach so that as we tell God's story, our listeners, and we ourselves, may find their place in it. One of my early mentors said, "Teaching has a subject; preaching has an object." The subject is faith. The object is to lead a listener to the jumping-off point of faith, and then give a little push.

The task of a preacher is not to tell us who we are, but to help us tell ourselves who we are. That means preachers are storytellers, for our identity comes to us in our stories, the ones we hear and the ones we tell.

Preachers are story-tellers. Pastors are story-listeners. It is our whole job, telling and listening. The two are never completely divided. We are never just preacher or just pastor. Even as we preach, we select the stories and the ways we tell them because of what we have heard in private, individually, from the persons who now sit before us, as a congregation. As we listen personally, pastorally, to individuals, we hear with ears that have been shaped by the stories of God in relationship to God's whole people.

My mother says that as a very small child, if I told her a fib, I would immediately blurt out, "That's a lie!" It's hard to have a very interesting childhood if you can't lie to your mother. Indeed, it's difficult to be a good storyteller if you feel bound to the "facts." It's a pretty good quality for a preacher, though, to know that story and truth are one. What is true is story; what is false is not story.

In his novel, *Things Fall Apart*, Chinua Achebe tells of some African villagers who have heard tales of men with white skins, men who have sticks they can point at you and make you fall down dead, even if they are a long distance away. The villagers go to their wise man, their storyteller, their preacher, if you will, and say to him, "Such stories surely cannot be true." He replies, "There is no story that is not true."

When my conservative minister's friend said of me, "He's just a storyteller," he replied, "Exactly!" I couldn't have asked for a nicer compliment.

note

[1]Here's one about story shifting itself: A church member asked, "What do preachers do at those meetings and conferences they're always going to?" "They trade stories." "Hmmm . . . I think our preacher gets cheated."

when you're in the second row, @ll by yourself

Our older daughter's name is Mary, of course. Mary Beth. After she graduated from college and entered the work force, she joined a university church in her secular city. The church building is very large and very long, a modern Gothic edifice. It was built for a time when the 35,000 students who surround it filled it up three times on a Sunday morning. It is a faithful and creative congregation, but now it is only half-full twice on a Sunday.

It is the back half, of course, that is filled. Except for Mary Beth. She sits in the second row, all by herself. That's where the preacher's kids have always sat—the second row. So that's where Mary Beth sits, when she's not greeting or ushering or dancing in "The Word in Motion," the church's liturgical dance group.

Mary Beth had been a member there about a year when a strange thing happened. Right in the middle of the sermon, during the second service, this wild-haired and wild-eyed young man walked in. He was carrying a case of some sort. It might have contained a musical instrument; it might have held something else. He started walking down the middle aisle of this long and majestic church building, slowly, with measured stride. With each row he passed, the eyes of the people in that row turned in unison and followed him. Finally, the entire congregation had forgotten entirely about the sermon and was staring at the wild-eyed young man.

What was he doing there? Why was he walking down the aisle in the middle of the sermon? What did he have in the case? Was it a gun? Would he pull it out and start shooting, as mad people do in public places, in this uncivilized era when the right to own guns is more precious than the right to live?

My friend, Paul Unger, was the preacher. By chance, we were in a meeting together that week. He told me the story of the young man and said . . .

"By the time he'd gotten halfway up the aisle, I realized no one, except Mary Beth, was listening to the sermon anymore, so I simply stopped preaching and stood there in the pulpit, wondering what the ushers were going to do about this. I found out later that they were standing back there in the narthex wondering what I was going to do about it."

"When I stopped preaching, Mary Beth turned around and saw him. He was almost up to her row. He turned around and faced the congregation for a long time. I thought Mary Beth was going to charge him. Then he said, 'Lies, all lies,' and walked out the same way he had come."

I felt like I'd been pole-axed. I ran to a telephone and called Mary Beth.

"Paul Unger told me about what happened at church last Sunday."

"Yes, it was very strange."

"He said he thought you were going to charge the guy."

"Yes, I got ready to. I slipped off my shoes and pulled up my skirt and lined up my legs with the gap between the pews so I could get some traction to go after him. I figured if he had a gun in that case and pulled it out and started shooting, I was going for him."

I thought to myself, "Good grief, I've reared an idiot."

I said out loud, "My God, Mary Beth! You're 5'6" and weigh 120. You're 24 years old. Don't you know if he had a gun, he'd kill you before you ever got to him? You should have been hiding under a pew, not getting ready to charge a mad man!"

"But Daddy, you don't understand. I was the only person up there. Yes, I knew if he had a gun, he'd kill me before I could get to him. But I thought that might be just enough time for Paul to duck down in the pulpit, for the organist and choir to get out the side doors of the chancel, for the rest of the congregation to hide under the pews, for the ushers to go for help. I was in the second row, all by myself. In that place, at that moment, I was the only one. If anyone did anything, it was going to have to be me!"

Mary Beth is her own woman. She's forged her values in the furnace of her own experience, including the church. She's my daughter, too. I was the main preacher she listened to for her first 18 years. That was what she had heard from me—that when you're in the second row, all by yourself, you don't worry about saving your soul; you try to figure out how to save someone else's life. When there's a gap between love and hate, you throw your body into that gap. That is the message of the cross, isn't it? That's what I have tried to preach.

How is it possible to be so proud of a child, so aware that she has done you the compliment of taking your preaching seriously, and at the same time so much wish she'd never heard that message of what is necessary, when you're in the second row, all by yourself?

desperately ⓢeeking
Thorndyke

My wife fell in love with the bear. It was just one in Mary V.'s collection of 300, but it was the one for Helen. Throughout the week in California, she held it on her lap to watch TV, carried it around the house, tucked it in bed with a kiss each night. His name was Thorndyke, and I was a bit jealous.

When Mary V.'s husband, Richard Lindquist, died of kidney cancer in November of 1988, we went to California to be with her. I ended up doing his funeral, as I had their two youngest sons. I didn't want to do Dick's funeral, wasn't sure I could. He was a great guy, and I loved him. More importantly, he was my sister's husband, and she loved him. They had been through a lot together, and he had never failed her. When she asked me to preach his funeral, I remembered why I was in the ministry, how I had traded my life for hers. Now, once again, I had a chance to give her a gift no one else could.

That's one of the joys of ministry, giving gifts no one else can. One such gift, strangely, is a funeral. At a time when people struggle so hard to be helpful, and can find so few ways or words, I have a mighty gift to give. For my sister I would struggle through, to give her this gift.

Gift giving has been easier for me as a minister than as a husband. Ministers are often husbands, and sometimes husbands are ministers. Occasionally, the unique gifts ministers can give are useful even to wives, or husbands if the minister is a woman.

When Helen's mother, Georgia Karr, the world's greatest mother-in-law, died, her Presbyterian pastor was out of town. We arranged for the local United Methodist pastor to do her funeral at the Presbyterian church building. An hour before the service, he called and backed out. I preached

Georgia's funeral. I was glad I did. It was a gift I could give to her, and to the rest of her family, but, most importantly, to Helen.

Thankfully, the occasion for ministerial gifts to one's family are few. Minister-husbands, then, when they must give gifts, are left to fall back on the same time-honored qualities that other husbands use when selecting presents for their wives—ignorance, insensitivity, and bad taste.

While I was gifting my sister with a funeral for her husband, I was well aware that the need for other gifts was quietly sneaking up in a red and green suit. So I took the presence of Thorndyke in Mary V.'s house as a sign; I would secretly get Helen her own Thorndyke for Christmas.

My sister, of course, could not remember where she got the bear. No problem; he had identification. His tag said he was Thorndyke, from Classic Carousel of Eden Valley, Minnesota. Thus armed, I slipped out of the house each day in shorts and t-shirt to do "training runs" that were actually bear hunting treks. I asked for Thorndyke in every one of the several dozen teddy bear dens, toy shops, and variety stores within running distance of my sister's house—in those days for me, about 10 miles. No Thorndyke.

When I got home, I drove—to Champaign, to Decatur, to Springfield, to Mattoon, to Charleston. I put 200 miles on my bear-hunting 1978 GMC pickup, the one with the exploding sidesaddle gas tanks. Not only did no bear store or toy store or department store or gift store have a Thorndyke, they had never heard of Classic Carousel. One store, however, thought there was a company called Eden Toys.

So, the phone company not being on strike, I called information for Eden Valley, Minnesota. No listing for Eden Toys. None for Classic Carousel. None for Classic. None for Carousel. None for bears. When you need information about a business, where do you go?

"Give me the number of the Eden Valley Chamber of Commerce," I said.

"Are you kidding?" lilted the Norwegian operator. "Eden Valley only has 750 people!"

"Well, is there a Chamber of Commerce anywhere around there?"

"Paynesville's closest."

I had never heard of Paynesville, but it seemed to be appropriately named. I told her to go for it.

About 18 rings later a male voice said, rather hesitantly, "Hello?"

I told him my problem.

"Well, yes, I know which outfit you mean. Only one over there. Can't think of their name, though. I'll give you Harry's number. He's secretary of the Chamber. He'll know."

I called Harry and explained how I got his number

"Whothe_____ you talk to over there? You couldn't a talked to someone at the Chamber. I *am* the Chamber."

After we didn't get that straightened out, he said, "Sure. That's Animal Fair. Everybody knows that."

Back to information for the number of Animal Fair. Called them. 18 rings later a female voice said, rather hesitantly, "Hello?"

"Animal Fair?"

"Well . . . yes . . ."

"Do you make a Classic Carousel bear named Thorndyke?"

"Well . . . golly . . . I don't think I can answer that."

"You don't know what bears you have?"

"Well, here we just stuff them. We don't name them or sell them or anything. But I'll give you a number to call."

It was a New York area code. I called. I explained.

"You'll have to talk to customer service," the woman said.

"John" came on the line. I explained again.

"What size Thorndyke you want?"

"Different sizes?"

"Sure," he said. "Little, Medium, Big"

"My wife's 5'4", and when she dances with it, it puts its legs around her waist."

"Got to be the big one," he assured me.

"Good," I said. "Send me a big one."

"Well, I can't do that. I'll have to give you Sue Beanblossom's number. She's our representative in your area. She can tell you which stores have them."

"You mean you have different representatives for different sizes of Thorndyke?" I asked.

Why else would he need to know the size? John hung up.

I knew a call to Sue Beanblossom would not be the end. She had a (312) area code. That's Chicago. (312) people do not do things for (217) people. But I called her.

"Oh, my representative in your area is Edith Raven," said Sue.

I called Edith.

"Ja," she said. "Ich habe viele teddy bears."

"Gut," I replied. "Ich brauche ein teddy bear heise Thorndyke."

It was only then that the true spiritual nature of this quest dawned on me; I was speaking in tongues.

"Wait, Edith," I cried. "I can't carry on about teddy bears in a foreign language. I just want a big Thorndyke for my wife's Christmas present."

"Oh, yes, ha-ha," said Edith. "I forget where I am, and I speak zee wrong vey. You go to Champaign. You go to Pages for All Ages."

"But Edith! That's not a bear store. It's a bookstore. I was just in there two days ago buying a Michener book. They're really nice there; two of the clerks helped me carry it to my truck. I didn't see any bears."

"Ja, dat ees problem mit dat bookstore. Too nice. Zee peoples read zee books. Don' see zee bears."

I called Pages for All Ages.

"I want a big Thorndyke," I told the woman who answered.

"The big one? I don't think it's for sale. I think it's just for display in the store. When Sue, the owner, comes in, I'll have her call you."

"Don't bother," I said. "Just tell her Valdez is coming." (I've always been a big Elmore Leonard fan.)

Sue was there when I arrived.

"Oh, we can't sell him," she said. "He sits there in the children's section, and they hug him and read stories to him. The children would be brokenhearted if we sold him."

"I've got to have one. Can't you order me one?"

"Well, two is the minimum order now. But one of the girls said another man, Valdez or something, called about a Thorndyke this morning. Maybe he'll come in and buy the other one."

I know I should have told her about Valdez, but . . . I was sure she would have no trouble selling plenty of Thorndykes.

Then another bulb came on above her head.

"Do you know how much a big Thorndyke costs?"

I thought about the mileage, my singular support of Ma Bell, the days away from work while desperately seeking Thorndyke . . .

"I don't care how much it costs," I snarled. "Just get me that bear."

She recited the price of the bear as if in prayer. The sales tax alone could pay Rush Limbaugh's dessert bill for a week. I gave her my credit card. Then I went home and tried to figure out how I could sell the car for more than it was worth.

They called two days before Christmas. The voice said simply, "He's here." I jumped in the truck and soon was in the back room of Pages for All Ages, looking down into a box that could have doubled for a burial vault. It was him, for sure; no mistaking that silly grin. They wrapped the box in a red and green circus tent. I took it home and slipped it under the tree.

Helen tried and tried to guess. She shook and rattled and rolled the box. She questioned our children. Nothing provided even an inkling. I hadn't felt so proud since I was 18 months old and ate the whole stick of butter and was sure my mother wouldn't notice.

On Christmas morning Helen ripped open the box with her Swiss Army knife. With a squeal, she started pulling Thorndyke from his cardboard bed. She pulled and pulled and pulled some more. Finally he was out.

He was enormous! Twice as big as my sister's! They told me the wrong size! The grizzlies on PBS are nothing compared to Thorndyke. I could have saved the car ...

Now he sits in a Boston rocker in the living room, his flat-top hidden by a red and white Indiana University cap. Except, of course, when the Chicago Bears are playing football; then he comes out to the family room and sits in front of the TV and grins and grunts and yells, "Where's that big bear Butkus?" He learned that from Helen.

I've wondered a good bit about why I want to put this story in this book. It's a fun story, but does it have something to do with ministry? Not really, except to note that ministers are called not so much to preach about love as to love. Far higher and more noble than my call to ministry is my call to love. Helen has been given to me by God as my opportunity to respond to the call to love. The search for Thorndyke is a furry symbol of what it means to answer the call of love. If I ever had to choose between the ministry and Helen, there would be no choice at all. I know which is the high calling.

note

[1]Known now for contemporary cop and adventure novels, Leonard, the best dialogue writer around, was originally a Westerns writer. Perhaps even better than *Hombre* is *Valdez Is Coming*.

the call to either/or

It's a strange thing, but we get healed only if we are sick, become whole by being broken. Jesus talked about this, probably more times than are reported in the Gospels. "The well have no need of a physician," he said, "only the sick."

I was sick. At first I thought it would pass. A little pain is to be expected after an evening of eating corn chips and chocolate-covered peanuts and listening to good preachers tell bad jokes. The pain, however, kept getting worse.

I couldn't go to church, even though it was World Communion Sunday. Helen called a retired pastor friend, Max White, to come lead the worship and serve communion. It was only the second time in 34 years of ministry that I had missed a worship service because of illness. Worse, I couldn't go to the Indiana University-University of Illinois basketball game that afternoon in Champaign, even though daughter Katie, an IU undergraduate but now an Illinois graduate student in history, had stood in line six hours to get tickets. Helen said, "I didn't worry too much when you missed church, but I knew you were sick when you couldn't go to the basketball game." The game was to be my birthday present. Instead, my present turned out to be a surgeon's scalpel.

They took me into the operating room at midnight. At 3:00 AM the surgeon told my wife that a tumor had penetrated the wall of my bowel. That was what was causing the pain. He was reasonably sure it was malignant.

I knew nothing of the surgeon's grim news to Helen in that tired hour. Certainly cancer had not occurred to me as I waited on the sterile metal operating table, thanking the nurses and technicians for coming in to work on me in the middle of the night.

There was no reason to suspect cancer. Even though my mother is one of eight children and my father one of seven,

and I thus have about a hundred cousins, there was no cancer in my entire family when I got sick. More than that, I'd
had no symptoms at all. We live a healthy lifestyle. Helen is a
professional home economist; she knows about diet. I could
run 26 miles, play third base. I'm a *minister*, for God's sake! I
don't get sick; I comfort other people when they get sick.

I woke up some time the next day and made a bad mistake. I counted the tubes in and out of my body. There were
more tubes than I had openings for tubes. They'd made new
holes in my body so they could put all their tubes in! I began
to understand why they all wore masks.

I had been cut open from Los Angeles to Boston. It
wasn't that I couldn't move without pain; I simply couldn't
move. I had a "belly buddy," just a rolled-up blanket to hold
over my incision if I felt I had to cough or sneeze, which I
was strongly advised not to try. Still, when the Nazi nurses
discovered I was awake, they unhooked all my tubes and
hauled me out of bed and told me to start walking. I got as
far as the door.

I was in the hospital for almost two weeks, getting my
tubes unhooked at 5:00 every morning so I could stand on
the scales, then getting back into bed and getting them all
hooked up again, trying to blow little plastic balls up little
plastic tubes, going much longer without washing my hair
than I ever thought possible, walking a little farther down
the hall each day, dragging on wheeled poles all the bottles
and tubes and machines and walls and beds and people that
were attached to me, eating nothing, getting stronger and
weaker at the same time.

Sometime in that span of days, very early in the morning, a man I have since come to think of as "the pale
oncologist" came into my room. It seems to me it was the
very next morning after my surgery. Helen says it was a couple of days after that. It was, at least, the first morning my
anesthesia-fogged brain could remember.

He did not introduce himself, by name or by position. He was wearing a stethoscope around his neck, so I supposed he might be a physician. In the hospital, however, a stethoscope isn't an automatic identifier. Even custodians and cafeteria workers wear them, the latter, I suspect, to test the meat and sometimes the vegetables they put on the trays.

He stood at the foot of my bed, up against the wall, as far away from me as he could get. Jesus, nailed to a tiny cross on the wall of my room in this Catholic hospital, looked over his shoulder at me.

"Well, you've got it," said the pale oncologist. "I'll call the National Cancer Institute on Monday to see if there's any adjuvant therapy we can get you on, but I doubt it."

He then assumed the classic doctor's hospital pose—hand on the door, one foot in the air, ready for get-away.

There was too much anesthesia left in my brain. I couldn't understand him. "It?" What was "it?" Sounded like we were in a game of some sort and I'd been tagged, but who had tagged me, and why? "Adjuvant therapy?" Did this have something to do with the adjuvant general? I have the best vocabulary in Douglas County, Illinois, but I didn't know that word. (So, it's a small county, but it's still a pretty good achievement!)

"Wait," I said. "What's this 'it'?"

"Why cancer, of course," he said, his hand still on the knob. "I wouldn't be calling the NCI if you didn't have cancer."

That made sense, would have made it a little sooner if my brain had been functioning normally.

Cancer? But there was no cancer in my family. . . . I'd had no symptoms. . . . You *die* from cancer!

"Wait," I said, one more time. "What are my chances?"

It was several weeks before I heard the words he actually said. Every preacher knows that what is heard is far more important than what is said. What I heard at that moment was, "You will be dead in one to two years." Later, I realized that his words were, "You have a 70% chance of recurrence in one to two years." 70% sounded a lot like reality. Recurrence sounded a lot like death.

Wendy Harpham, a young medical doctor who is herself a cancer patient, tells the story of two duck hunters. One shot 10 feet in front of the duck. One shot 10 feet behind the duck. On the average, the duck was dead.

That's the problem with statistics and percentages. It was a long time before I understood that they are not useful to us. My chances are 100%, one way or the other, and so are those of every other cancer person. There is no such thing as 10% survival or 70% recurrence. Diagnoses and percentages put limitations on us. Cancer, however, is a very individual disease, and the percentages are always 100, but I did not know that then, in the presence of the pale oncologist.

He tried the knob again. This time, I let him go.

My first thought was, "But I can't even use up all my return address labels in two years." I didn't realize it at the time, but that was a good sign. I was going for the two, the longest option I was given.

Then I began to assess my life. I had walked neither of my daughters down the aisle. I had not played trotty-horse with my grandchildren. Still, it had been a good life. I had experienced all the important things—love. But it seemed so short, like a fragment of a life, not a whole life, like a spark from a flint that had not yet caught fire.

Also, it seemed so wasteful. Not like the prodigal son, certainly. I had been true to my call, as I understood it. I had studied hard, worked even harder, been highly responsible, always put the needs of others ahead of myself. I had taken up my cross daily and done my best to follow Jesus, sacrificed time and energy and material goods. I had preached the good news.

That, of course, was the problem. I had preached the good news, but I hadn't lived by it. What made my life so wasteful and wasted was that I hadn't had a good time. Why would God call someone to a life that didn't include having a good time? After all, Jesus said he came that we might have not just life, but abundant life. I had heard of that call, especially in "The Year of Sandinistas," but still I hadn't heard it for my own life. Was that my true calling, the call I had failed to hear and to heed? When I had traded my life for my sister's, was it to a life of joy that I was trading?

Even then, it didn't occur to me to use my last two years to have a good time. I had 19 file drawers of materials I'd accumulated over the years, mostly for sermons I would one day preach or articles or books I would someday write. I went home to continue serving my congregation, to put aside as much money as possible for Helen for when I was gone, and to clean out my file drawers. In my mind I had the idea that perhaps some of that stuff could be salvaged, to be passed along to younger preachers for their use. In my heart I knew better. All those clippings and great ideas would have to return to ashes, along with me. That was the last gift I would give my wife, five empty file cabinets.

In the meantime, before I went home to throw out accumulated stuff, two other especially significant events occurred in the hospital. The pale oncologist returned, and my surgeon didn't.

The pale oncologist returned once, briefly, to tell me there wasn't any adjuvant therapy for my type of cancer, that it would be necessary for me just to look over my shoulder to see if they were gaining on me. It didn't sound like a very good time.

After a week or so, I began to get sick again, this time from weakness. I was on a "clear liquid" diet, which consisted mainly of grape juice that was strained through nuclear waste, to give it that particularly tangy taste. After several mornings of hugging my belly buddy close while the grape juice came back up and made a pallid imitation of Lenten stoles on my limp front, the head nurse told me,

"Oh, by the way. Don't drink that grape juice. It always makes everybody sick."

"Why do you give it to us," I asked, "if it makes us sick?"

"Oh, we don't give it to you. That comes from downstairs."

"Don't they have telephones downstairs? Don't you know anybody down there you could talk to? Couldn't someone ride the elevator down there and tell them not to send it up anymore? Couldn't you take if off the trays before you bring it in?"

She left, a little miffed, I think, that I wasn't more appreciative of her warning.

It had been about 12 days, and I had lost 20 pounds. I knew this from the 5:00 AM weigh-ins.

"Why do you get me up to weigh me?" I asked the genial male nurse one morning. "You know I've lost some more, because you never give me anything to eat."

"Have a good day," he said when he left.

I didn't have a good day, but Thorndyke sailed through it with his usual ease. Helen had brought her huge teddy bear to the hospital to keep me company. She had dressed him in a hospital gown and put a bandage on his paw. He was taking the hospital experience with greater dignity than I could muster, and as usual, I was a bit jealous of him. Still, I appreciated his presence, because the nurses loved him. I got a little extra attention because they stopped in to see him whenever they passed our room. Some even checked his vitals. There was a rumor that he had his own chart in the third-shift party room, which doubled as the nurses' station. It was conveniently located right outside my door, where I could smell brownies and popcorn all night.

When Paula, the night nurse, came on, she came in, as usual, to grab Thorndyke and hug him 'til he popped.

"Paula, I'm starving," I told her.

"Sorry. How are you tonight, honey bear? Can't give you anything to eat. Oh, I love you so much. You're on clear liquids. You're just so cute. When the doctors write some new orders, we'll move you up to full liquids, then to a regular diet. I hope your paw's getting better."

I wasn't exactly sure which of us she was talking to, and I didn't know exactly what "full liquids" meant, but it sounded marvelous.

"Well, how can they write any new orders? They haven't been in for three days."

That got her attention. She actually put Thorndyke down and looked at me.

"Three days?"

I sensed for the first time in this hospital experience, I had some sort of advantage. I pushed it.

"Yes, maybe even longer. I'm so weak, I can't remember very well."

That got her on a roll, out the door. I could hear her talking on the phone. She rolled back in.

"You can have anything you want!"

"Anything?"

"That's what they said. Of course, the kitchen's closed, and all we have is ice cream bars and graham crackers."

"Exactly what I was hoping for. Bring 'em on. But how come I can suddenly move to 'anything I want' without going through full liquids and all that?"

"Well, I think they're a little bit embarrassed. Your doctors forgot you're in the hospital."

Forgot? My surgeon forgot me? How could that be? I was in the hospital, lying there, waiting for someone to take care of me, to make me well, and they simply forgot about me, forgot I was even there!

There was a reasonable explanation for the surgeon's absence. He had left on vacation immediately after operating on me. While he was gone, his partner called on me. When my original surgeon returned, the partner understandably thought he no longer needed to call on me, so he stopped, and . . . Well, maybe it's a reasonable explanation, although I didn't get any help in figuring it out. The surgeon came in the next day to say I could go home as soon as I could keep a regular meal down and have a bowel movement. He didn't mention anything about forgetting me.

He did good surgery. I can hardly see the scar now. He may have done more for my long-term survival, though, by forgetting me than by operating on me. Bernie Siegel says that 15% of cancer patients are automatic fighters. They fight anything, and cancer's just another duck on the line. Another 15% are automatic diers. If the doctor says they have six months to live, they'll die exactly six months later. The 70% in between can be taught to fight. I suspect I was in the upper half of that 70%.

It was my surgeon's forgetfulness that started me on the way to taking care of myself rather than waiting for someone else to do it. I didn't come to the full realization at that moment, in the hospital, but slowly I understood: "*I'm* the doctor!" I'm the one responsible for my own health. I need the assistance of surgeons and oncologists and nurses and technicians, but it's my body and my life. I'm the one who has to keep good watch and make good decisions.

In the meantime, though, I was still depressed, by the general anesthesia in my cells, and by the throwaway phrase of the pale oncologist. I didn't know I was depressed. Anesthesia is like that.

I went home, not to fight, but to clean out drawers and to look over my shoulder.

Then my wife and daughters began to protest. So did a few friends. Chief among them was Rose Mary Shepherd. I had been Rose Mary's pastor in my previous church when she went through cancer.

"You can't just take this lying down," she said. "Get a second opinion. Go to my oncologist."

More to please Rose Mary than anything else, I did.

"I do think there's an adjuvant therapy for you," he said. "We have a new protocol for colon cancer. In fact, we're

participating in a clinical trial out of the Mayo Clinic. You'd
have 12 months of chemotherapy. The only problem is, you
have to start within 30 days of your surgery, and today is
your 30th day. Why don't you go out in the waiting room,
have a donut, talk it over with your wife."

I was on my way out, in the doctor's pose, hand on the
knob, when he added, "Oh, by the way . . . I have to go to a
board meeting in 15 minutes, so come back before I leave."

I wandered through the rows of look-alike hallways until
I finally came to the waiting room. I shuffled over to the
refreshments table. All the donuts were gone! The one thing
in the day I had to look forward to, and it wasn't going to
happen. This wasn't a good sign.

I sat down, donutless, beside Helen, in the company of
20 strangers in orange chairs.

"For what it's worth," she said very softly, so only I could
hear, "I know what I'd do if it were my body."

But that was the problem! This wasn't *my* body! My
body played third base. My body ran marathons. My body
made love. My body ate prodigious quantities of pumpkin
pie. I'd been put into some other body, a feeble and puny
body, a hunched-over body, an aching body, a body with so
much of its insides gone that it had to hang around the
bathroom for four hours every morning because it had to sit
on the throne five times in those four hours and got only
about 15 seconds notice before each regal occasion.

Of course, that made the decision easier. It wasn't my
body, so who cared what happened to it? I had pastored
enough people going through chemotherapy that I should
have had no illusions about its ill effects. They, however,
were in their own bodies. I wasn't worried; I wasn't in mine.

I got back to my new oncologist before he left for his
meeting. He sent me out to the front desk, where, I learned
over the next year, some of the friendliest and kindest people
in the world resided. They told me to wander through the
halls again and look for a cute little redhead with a great

laugh. That turned out to be Kim Wagler, an oncology nursing specialist. She showed us a video, told us about potential
side effects, and gave me my first treatment.

The drugs were leukevorin, levamisole, and 5FU. Leukevorin is a vegetable abstract that lessens the symptoms of
the active drugs. 5FU is the granddaddy of all cancer drugs,
the one that makes you lose your hair and your lunch.
Levamisole is a sheep worm medicine. It's been around a
long time. The sheep farmers in my congregation can go to
the local Farm and Fleet store and buy the exact same medicine for their sheep for one cent on the dollar of what it
costs a cancer patient. No one has yet explained to me why
sheep get it cheaper.

Have you ever wondered how they discover that a sheep
worm medicine is a cure for colon cancer? Apparently these
two oncologists are driving down the interstate and see a
flock of sheep in a field.

"You know, Al, those sheep look mighty healthy."

"You're right, Pat. Let's stop and ask that farmer what
he's giving those sheep, and we'll give the same stuff to our
colon cancer patients, and the drug companies can charge
them a hundred times as much."

That's the way I imagine it, anyway. At least I no longer
have to worry about my lifelong phobia of getting sheep
worms!

I drove the 70-mile round trip to the cancer center each
day, Monday through Friday, and then had three weeks off.

On the first Friday I said to Kim: "I'm not really a side-
effects kind of guy. I know you told me about all that might
happen because you have to, but I've taken this stuff for five
days now, and nothing. I think I'll get through this without
any of that stuff."

Oh, yes, most certainly, "Pride goes before a fall." It
began on Saturday. By Sunday morning my lips were red
and puffy, and sores had begun in my mouth. My eyes had
sealed themselves shut with some sort of secretion, and were

out of focus even after Helen washed them out and got them open. My hands and feet began to swell. I got through the worship service and collapsed. Helen got a little potato soup down me at lunch. The 5FU got it back up again. So went the week—nausea, swelling, eye problems, mouth sores . . . and incredible fatigue.

You can't really understand chemo fatigue without experiencing it. It's not just tiredness. You go to bed as tired as a bowl of soggy cornflakes and sleep 10 hours and get up as tired as two bowls of soggy cornflakes. About four years after my own experience I called on a member of my congregation who was going through chemo. "I've been lying here on the sofa for three hours," he said, "thinking about getting up and taking a shower." That sums it up; thinking about it is as far as you can go. During side-effects week my goal was to do one thing each day. The one thing might be a telephone call, or writing a letter, or—on a good day—doing the dishes. That was the most I could muster, and some days I didn't even manage the one thing.

During that week I longed for colored food. All I could eat was cottage cheese, potato soup, tapioca, saltines. Helen finally bought a set of colored dishes for me to use during "white week."

By the next Sunday the side effects would begin to wane. The second week I began to get my strength back. The third week I began to feel almost normal. Then we'd go back and do it all again.

The premise of chemotherapy is simple, and blunder-buss. Cancer cells are fast dividers. Simply put, that's why they create tumors; more cells are being created than there's room or jobs for, so they hang around on the street corners of the body and form gangs. Chemotherapy poisons and kills fast-dividing cells. Unfortunately, other fast dividers are on your head and in the lining of your gastrointestinal tract, etc. Thus the hair loss and nausea. The good fast-dividing cells are being poisoned, too. The hope is that the bad ones, the cancer cells, will stay dead, and the good ones will regenerate. In the meantime they all suffer, good and bad alike. "The rain," said Jesus, "falls on the just and on the unjust."

One April morning I ventured out from behind the red bricks of our house for a real walk, on sidewalks, under trees. Kim and the other nurses had told me, "When you feel tired, take a walk. It will do you more good than a nap." I wasn't sure the walks untired me, but the naps didn't either, and I was desperate to be out, to do something normal. Besides, it looked like a nice day for a walk.

A block away from my house it wasn't that nice. The bright spring day I had seen from my living room was a false spring day beyond my walls—sun shining, buds forming, but breezily chilling. I managed one more block and realized I had gone too far. I made a wide, slow, "don't pull anything" turn, hunched my head down into my shoulders and my hands up into my chest, and began to turtle my way home. With each step the tricky spring chill worked its way deeper into my depleted body. I started thinking about the houses on my way home, wondering if I knew anyone who would take me home in a car. Less than two blocks, and I needed a ride. Here was a man who two months earlier could run 26 miles, and now he couldn't walk four blocks!

Then I heard a voice. It said, "I'm thankful for the cancer." It was a strange voice, croaky from a week with a tube rubbing on its vocal chords, powerless because of severed diaphragm muscles, but it was remarkably like my voice. I knew that couldn't be. Why would I be thankful for cancer? The voice said it again. "I'm thankful for the cancer."

Why? Why would anyone be thankful for cancer? What could possibly be good about it? I didn't understand it, but once again, I heard a strange call.

This time I was called to an either/or ministry. Either I would get well, or I would die. I no longer had the energy to cover up my life with a blanket of churchly activities. My ministry was out in the open and down to the basics. Either

I would teach my people how a Christian lives, or I would teach them how a Christian dies. Either way, life or death, getting whole was my calling and my ministry.

get well, but only during office hours

There are grave dangers in the either/or ministry of teaching how to live or how to die through one's own life or death. Preachers can become very boring if they speak only of themselves and their own trials, give an "organ recital" each Sunday in the pulpit and each time someone makes the mistake of saying, "How are you?" I worked hard at avoiding that sort of self-centeredness. I tried to live and preach the gospel, not my current biography, but I used my own struggle toward wholeness as a moving picture of the drama in which we all must live, hearing and responding to the call of God.

This new ministry was not met with acclaim by all, and not just because I sometimes stepped beyond the barriers of good taste and too much self. Some people are so afraid of cancer, they don't even want to hear the word. Some folks think the best way to deal with any disease is to deny it. Some don't want to be bothered with your struggles and want you to act as though nothing is unusual, not for your benefit, but for their own.

One man in my congregation told me repeatedly about all the persons he had ever known who'd had cancer. There was one theme in all the stories: right up to the day they died, you never would have known they even had it. They went on with their lives as usual. His point was clear: I should go on with my life as usual, too, not bothering him or anyone else with the messy details of a broken life searching for wholeness, not reminding the church members that they might have to go through this sometime themselves. I should preach in front of them, pastor in front of them, lead the church in front of them. I should not get well in front of them, because getting well was an admission that I was sick.

Every cancer patient, regardless of their place in life, experiences the people who don't want to hear the word, who don't want you to give any indication you are sick, who want you—and everything else—to go as "normal." In addition to the demands put upon all cancer patients, cancerous ministers have another arrow to dodge.

People don't want to know that their pastors get sick, that they have sexual thoughts, that they are self-centered, that they can't or don't control their eating or drinking (even though Protestants encourage their pastors to eat too much, and Catholics encourage their priests to drink too much), that they need money to live on, that they get in debt, that they get tired, that there are people they don't like, that they don't want to call in nursing homes, that they'd rather fish or go to movies or run than read the Bible, that they get weary with committee meetings and confirmation classes and bazaars and suppers and the whole church thing!

Some people become very hostile when the minister shows any sign of weakness. They're like a pack of hyenas around a wounded lion. When the lion is still king of the jungle, because he's stronger and less fearful than all the other animals, they stay at a distance and mute their voices. When the lion has been tossed by an elephant and is bleeding and limping, however, they dash in, not only to grab a portion of the lion's kill before he can have his fill, but to yelp and bite at the lion himself, taunting, "Hey, who's so mighty now?"

Some ministers bring this on themselves. They stalk proudly through the jungle of the church, beating their breasts and proclaiming, "I am king of the jungle." When some female lion comes along and snips off that lion's mane and makes a monkey of him, he looks pretty stupid.[1]

There are ministers who claim they are nothing special. "I'm not a lion," they say. "I'm just a monkey, too. I only want to enable and empower the rest of you to be the best monkeys you can be." Congregations despise monkey pastors. They want lions. They don't want self-proclaimed lions, but they do want lions. They do not, however, want sick or tired lions. Unfortunately, for them and for their lions, even the king of the jungle eventually gets sick and tired and old.

There weren't very many hyenas in my church, although, as always, it was a rude surprise to learn there were any at all, and that there were more than I ever would have guessed, and exactly who they were. In most cases they were the very same people who had counted on me most in my lion role, those who consistently turned to me when they were them- selves sick, or family-torn, or out of work, or in despair. These folks can't stand to have a sick lion. It reverses the roles. That is too threatening.

Office hours became the symbol of that threat. Pre- viously, I had been in my office in the church building each morning from nine to noon. I hadn't announced these as office hours; I just showed up every day. That pattern quickly became known and accepted. It is assumed that ministers call in hospitals and nursing homes and on shut- ins in the afternoons and go to meetings or do counseling in the evenings. The only time left for the office is morning hours. Some church members dropped by the office on an almost daily basis, others only occasionally, usually not because they needed help, but just to say "hello," just to touch base and thus feel safe. "The minister is there if I need him. He's always there. I can count on him." I should have had a sign on my door saying, "The lion is in."

To deal with the bathroom effects and medicinal neces- sities of my semi-colon, I had to be up at five each morning to be in the office at nine. (For the first four hours each morning, my colon needs to be within 30 seconds of a bath- room.) To get up at five, I had to be in bed by nine the night before. It's almost impossible for a minister to be in bed by nine every night; there are church meetings that run later than that! Besides, eight hours was hardly enough rest to recover from surgery, and then deal with chemotherapy. There were days I threw up every 30 minutes; I wasn't even sure I could make it as far as the church bathroom when those needs "arose."

I explained all this to the congregation, and to many members individually, several times, in several settings, carefully. I explained that I would not be able to keep regular office hours, but that I would be available as much as possible. I gave my secretary instructions that if anyone came to the church office looking for me, she should telephone me and I would come right over, if I could physically. (We lived only half a block away.) I told the congregation that she had these instructions. I encouraged people to telephone me at home to make appointments to see me. I told them that if they needed to, they could just come directly to our house, appointment or not.

In this process I made three mistakes: I got sick. I assumed people would be sympathetic with my plight and would cut me the slack I needed. I explained the situation.

There was nothing I could do about #1. I suppose I should have known better on #2, but there's a natural human assumption that folks will at least be nice to you if you are in need. I really did know better. I'd grown up poor. I knew that most people don't take care of you, even extend sympathy, because you're poor, or handicapped, or victimized. Instead, they despise you for it.

Your very presence puts pressure on them to be better than they want to be, to share some of what they have. Also, you remind them that they might some day suffer your fate, and they don't want to hear it. So they say your poverty or your handicap or your status as a rape victim or battering victim or a robbery or shooting victim is your own fault. "Why don't you get a job?" "There are special programs for people in wheelchairs, and my taxes pay for them, so take care of yourself." "Dressing like that, what did you expect?" "Why did you marry that guy in the first place?" "Why didn't you have an alarm system or a gun?" "Why did you go into that part of town at night?"

In addition, I'd been a pastor in congregations and other church settings for 34 years. I knew about wounded lions from my own experience and that of many colleagues. I knew that people expect the lion to keep going, regardless, to keep bringing down the kills off which the rest of the pack can feed. I should have known there would be pack members who resented my new disability.

Then, there was #3—explanation. I don't know how many ministers have gotten into trouble by explaining things, but I suspect it's about 100%.

I've come to the conclusion that a minister should never announce office hours. People want you on the job 24 hours a day, and that includes in the office in the church building. You're better off if you go along with that myth of total availability. If you announce there are certain hours you are available, that means there are other hours you aren't.

I recall too vividly my mistake when I first went to be Directing Minister of a large, multi-pastor church. In a church newsletter I explained that I wanted people to know when and where they could find me, so I announced what hours I would be in the office at the church. It seemed logical; if there were certain hours I would be there, people could find me more easily.

In this case, not only did the excrement hit the fan, but I *was* the fan. It was a university city, and most people were quite familiar with the concept of office hours. Many were amused at the furor and laughed it off. It was no laughing matter to the offended, however. These were primarily the fans and supporters of my predecessor, who were already unhappy that I was not he. (That's always a problem in any pastoral succession, but that's a story for a different time.)

My predecessor understood the congregational mind far better than I did. In fact, he had told me that he made it a point to be the first person in the building each morning and the last person out at night. He actually unlocked the place and relocked it, even though that was part of the custodian's job description! During his pastorate he mentioned his schedule, presumably in passing, often. In sermons he spoke of how beautiful the sunrise was when he arrived on Thursday morning, how calm the night was when he left on Monday evening. Quickly the myth took hold: he was there all the time!

The church secretary was a great fan of Reverend Allhours and didn't care much for me, but she laughed about it, too, when people began to criticize me for not being in the office enough, especially as compared to Reverend Allhours.

"You're actually here more than he was, and you're more available, because you tell me where you are when you aren't here. He arrived first and left last, but in between he just did quick ins and outs, and I never knew where he was. When people dropped by to see him, I'd tell them he'd been here earlier, and he'd be back, but he was out calling right now. I usually didn't know where he was, but I always said he was calling. How could anyone argue with that? He was *always* here, *except* when someone came by, and then he was calling on someone. Most people drop by maybe once a year. He wasn't here when they came, but they assumed he was here every hour of every other day, that he was out just that one time. Essentially, *he* told them he was always here, except when he was gone. *You* tell them you're never here, except when you're here. You're here more, but they think you're here less."

I remember the lady who came storming into my office one day to announce, "You need to be in the office more, and you need to be out calling more." I explained to her that I seemed to be in the office enough, and at the right time, since she had found me there, and that the two things she wanted were contradictory. She looked perplexed for a moment and then harrumphed, "Well, you ought to do it anyway!" Lions aren't supposed to have the limitations of normal creatures in the jungle.

I think my predecessor had the right idea. It's better just to assume, and let other people assume, that you are in the office all the time, except when some emergency takes you away. Don't announce hours; that puts a limit on. If you're not there, leave a note, or instruct the secretary to explain that you had to leave for awhile.

I should never have explained about my disability. I should have just showed up when I could, and when I couldn't, called in sick. I should have gone with the myth that I was always in the office, even though I was sick. If someone came by and the secretary said, "He's sick today," even if for the third straight day, that's very different from announcing ahead of time that you know you'll be sick, that you don't intend to be in the office.

Another problem with explanations is that folks don't hear them. Some never understood my problems, even with repeated explanations. Our men's group met for breakfast once a month on a Sunday morning at 7:30. Since our worship service started at 9:30, I *really* needed all my Sunday morning time to prepare physically for worship. There were at least two men who said to me four or five different times, "Say, you're not coming to the men's breakfast anymore. You ought to be coming." Each time I explained why I couldn't. Each time they seemed to understand. In two or three months, however, they'd be back with, "Say, you're not coming . . ."

My absence from the office became a cause for eight or ten people in the congregation. Their campaign started while I was still recovering from surgery and beginning chemotherapy. It was well known that the pale oncologist had pronounced a deadline of "a year or two" on me. Nonetheless, in the second month of what might be my last year on this earth, two of them went to the District

Superintendent to complain that I wasn't in the office enough!

They never gave it up. It became a yearly ritual at the charge conference (congregational meeting) for them to come in organized force and to move that I not be granted a salary raise for the coming year. When pressed for the reason, it was like the response to a litany: "He's not in the office enough." When others tried to explain that I was always available, even to the extent of coming to the office immediately if someone asked for me, they just shook their heads. When asked if there were anything else wrong with my performance, they'd say: "No, he's a good preacher, good pastor, great with funerals and weddings, the children like him, attendance is up, stewardship is better, but he's just not in the office enough."

Not surprisingly, but still strangely, they picked the moments when I was most vulnerable to press their attack. The charge conference at which they almost succeeded in denying a salary raise was the winter my parents were living with us so we could care for my father while he underwent two cancer surgeries of his own. I was distracted with care and concern for my parents. Sensing that, they pressed the charge. As Lee said of Grant's tactics, "They just keep coming."

This was a fiscally conservative congregation. Their idea of a merit raise was a minimal cost-of-living adjustment. Like basketball refereeing, in the ministry you're expected to start out perfect and get better as you go along. I was expected to earn the cost of living raise by doing a better-than-excellent job. "Better than excellent" was the standard. Since it's difficult to get much higher on the scale, an actual merit increase was never really a possibility, or even a consideration. We weren't talking about an actual raise, nothing to break the bank, or the budget. The yearly drag through the flint mine had nothing to do with whether there was money in the bank, only whether there was a body in the office.

Almost any minister will tell you that the hardest blow to your solar plexus doesn't come from the people who kick you in it, even when you're already bent over with pain and they catch you by surprise with steel-toed shoes. A minister's greatest disappointment comes from the "good" people of the church who stand by while "the children of darkness" sneak around planning their mischief. In fact, the good people stand by not only while the children of darkness plan their mischief, but while they carry it out and gloat over it later. The "good" people, who are usually 99% of the congregation, "just don't want to get involved," "feel that we shouldn't take sides," tell you privately that they're all for you but refuse to speak up at meetings, or even to come to the meetings. What they're really saying is, "You'll be gone some day, but we'll still be here, and so will your attackers. We have to continue to live with them. We're not willing to get on their wrong side just to defend you." It's a very understandable position.

When it comes to attack time, the minister is almost always entirely alone. Sounds like Jesus on the cross, doesn't it? So why are we always so surprised?

I'm not quite as naive as I may appear here. I understand why church members act as they do under given circumstances.[2] When people bring out their placards and their slogans about "office hours," they're really marching and chanting about attention and fear and doubt and, finally, God.

Maybe this is something the "good" people are right about. Maybe they're not supposed to be involved, lest the point be blunted. This isn't a church fight; it's a theological struggle with the devil. If God really called Jesus to climb up on Golgotha all alone, might God not also call me to stand on that little molehill called "office hours" all alone, precisely because that's the way God does things—one called person at a time? Who knows? I don't. I just try to be faithful to my strange calling. Sometimes I succeed.

Despite the office worshipers, I was fortunate. There were some in my congregation who were LPNs and RNs and MDs in lion care. Others weren't accomplished at pastoral care, in the sense of caring for the pastor, but they meant well. Ministry colleagues and friends from outside the church loved me and cared about me, sick as I was. In the midst of it all, I still said, "I'm thankful for the cancer." I still had a ministry, a ministry of getting whole.

notes

[1] I apologize to women ministers for this image. I do not intend to exclude you. I just couldn't figure a way to make the lion image gender-inclusive.

[2] It's not hard; just read Edwin Friedman's *Generation to Generation: Family Process in Church and Synagogue* (New York and London: Guildford Press, 1985).

now that i have c@ncer
i am whole

Two years looked pretty good, compared to one. That was the span the pale oncologist had given me, so I decided to try for the two.

One morning in side-effects week I was sitting on the couch in our living room when a big tour bus waddled by on our brick street. We lived in Amish country, so tour buses were as common as buggies. That's when my revelation came. I might not have even one year, let alone two. I could get run over by a tour bus this very day!

It's hard to explain what good news that was. I wasn't bound by the ties of the cancer or the deadline of the cancer doctor! I might not die from cancer at all. There were a hundred other deaths that might get me. A rabid squirrel could bite me. A runaway Amish horse could kick me in the head. Maybe a heart attack or a stroke. Most of all, a tour bus could run over me.

If a tour bus could run over me, then my task was not to get cured, but to get healed, to be whole. To quote Bernie Siegel again, "Not everyone will be cured, but everyone can be healed." The only way you can be sure you're ready to die, since you don't know when that moment of the bus will be, is to be whole all the time. There will always be unfinished "doing" business, but the time for concluding all one's "being" business is now.

I had lived a good life, but I hadn't lived it as a human being. Instead, I was a human doing. My reason and meaning for life came from hard work, good work, useful work —always work, always the doing. Now I couldn't do. I was too sick and too tired and too scared. Now, I could only be. It was time to become a human being, time to get whole. It was time to learn that, yes, faced with death on a calendar, I really do believe all the stuff I've been preaching all these years.

I'd like to tell you that I became some sort of a great spiritual person and my congregation was so inspired by my influence toward wholeness that they all became great spiritual persons, too. I didn't, and they didn't. A ministry of doing is a much easier ministry than a ministry of being. Still, I can't say just how, but I think I've been a better minister as a being than I was as a doing.

We worked at it, the ministry of being, day by day, trying to learn, trying to be kinder to one another, trying not to sweat the small stuff, trying to listen better for the word of God. We tried to remind each other of the good news that any one of us might get hit by a tour bus at any time. We worked at loving and being. Sometimes we did it pretty well; other times we didn't. Maybe that's what wholeness and ministry and the strange calling are all about. You can learn more about this by reading my book *Now That I Have Cancer I Am Whole: Meditations for Cancer Patients and Those Who Love Them*. Some things have happened since that book was published, though.

In that book I wrote about Becky Elliott, the head nurse in my cancer center, and how she always made me sick. Becky's a delightful and pretty woman, but I'd walk into the cancer center, take one look at her, and start calling Ralph on the big white phone. My brain knew that what she was going to do to me would make me sick, and my insides apparently figured they might as well get a jump on it. In September of 1995 I performed Becky's wedding. When she asked me to do it, I told her not to wear a white dress, considering what had always happened before when I saw her in white. "My pearls will protect me," she said. They did. After the wedding she thanked me for being there, and I thanked her for keeping me alive so I could be there, and we both cried. It was great fun.

Kim Wagler, my first chemo nurse, was diagnosed with breast cancer a few months after my diagnosis. We nursed and pastored each other through the years that followed. We continue to monitor and encourage each other, by telephone and in person. In May of 1996 I performed Kim's wedding. Becky was a guest, as Kim had been at Becky's wedding.

Helen says I'll probably be the only cancer patient in history who ends up doing weddings for all his nurses. It's a record I'll be glad to have.

On the fifth anniversary of my surgery the dreaded Dr. Bonello, my proctologist, shook my hand and said, "Congratulations! You're cured!"

I still believe that healing is more important than cure, but cure is a good word, too.

love and baseball

One of my first childhood memories is of Crosley Field in Cincinnati, sometime before World War II. My father's bachelor brothers took me to a game there when I was only three or four.

We all lived together in a big house on the edge of Oxford, Ohio. We called it Cedar Crest. Grandma and Grandpa Mac. Sometimes Uncle Harvey and Aunt Helen, my father's only sister, and their daughter, Elizabeth Anne. Sometimes Uncle Glen and Aunt Mable, too, with their daughters, Joan and Patty. (For a few years as a young adult, Patty was a circus performer; I still think of that as the highlight of our family history.) And the uncles, just teenaged boys—Bob, Randall, Mike. Only Uncle David and Aunt Ella Mae lived away during all the years at Cedar Crest, in Dayton. World War II hadn't started yet. The economy hadn't "recovered" yet. Uncle Rufus, Grandpa's brother, and Aunt Anna, Rufus' wife, lived in Oxford, too. Aunt Anna was the town telephone operator and knew things she never told.

It was at Cedar Crest that Mary V. and the cousins and I played store with things we had taken from Grandma's room. When Grandma got home from cleaning rooms at Western College, she'd come to the small barn, where we had set up our store, carefully pick through her belongings, as though trying to decide what she needed, and buy them back from us.

It was at Cedar Crest that I first listened to Uncle Rufus' stories of Edd Roush, of how they had grown up together in Oakland City, Indiana, playing baseball, dreaming of the majors. At 5'3", Uncle Rufus intended to be the shortest man in the Majors. Unfortunately, the Majors didn't want a left-side infielder who really was a short stop.

It was at Cedar Crest that I first learned to hit a baseball, with the teenage uncles pitching to me.

It was at Cedar Crest that I first learned God loves us. I suppose it was inevitable that I became a preacher. After all, if the first thing you learn is that God loves you, it's the only thing worth talking about for the rest of your life. Love and baseball.

It was at Cedar Crest that I learned God loves baseball. Grandma loved baseball. Even when they were old ladies, Grandma and Aunt Nellie, Grandpa's "old maid" sister, would get on the train and go down to Cincinnati on Ladies Day. Grandma loved baseball, and she loved me, and since God loved me, that meant God had to love baseball, too. I was sure that God would not want to get shown up in the love department by Grandma.

All I remember about that first game at Crosley is a green seat and purple pop and how excited the uncles were about what happened when the ball was hit, and the good feeling of being with people who loved me and loved base-ball, enough to put us together, in a place called Crosley, with a crowd of people even bigger than at church.

Now, in August of 1990, Katie and I drive up to Blue Ash, Ohio, to see the recreated Crosley Field, with the real scoreboard still showing the results of the last game there. Real Crosley seats, too, and a real ticket booth. Even the out-field terrace is supposed to be there, although I doubt it's original! The Crosley of Blue Ash is supposed to look almost like the old park, even the same dimensions, although not nearly as many seats, of course; it's just part of the city recreation park.

We assume that Blue Ash is a small town and we can ask at the corner gas station and be told immediately how to get to Crosley. Instead, the international headquarters of every Fortune 500 company, plus a few worldwide conglomerates, are crammed into a mass of sprawling, suburban business park buildings of a dozen floors each. Floors, not stories. It's hard to imagine stories being able to exist in such sites. The stories are in sights like Crosley. No one in Blue Ash, however, seems to have heard of it, even though articles about the restoration of the old field have appeared in regional and national publications.

Eventually one man at a corner gas station, which has 24 gas pumps and a supermarket, thinks he can direct us to it. His words include a couple of turns in the wrong direction, but we are good wanderers. Besides, we enjoy looking into people's garages as we turn around in their driveways. Finally we ask a letter carrier. They get mail there, so he knows where it is.

Katie and I park behind the scoreboard. Fortunately, we continue our Blue Ash disorientation and go in by the wrong way, slipping under a rail out in right field. If we had gone in the correct way, we would have seen the signs that say no one is allowed on the field. What use is a restored Crosley if you can't walk up the terrace to the scoreboard and pose there for a picture, taken by a daughter who's working on a doctorate, but who knows that baseball is what counts? Katie sets aside her dissertation research for three hours each summer's day to listen to Marty and Joe and the ghost of Waite Hoyt.[1]

We sit for a while in the green seats of old Crosley. We take off our shoes. This, after all, is holy ground. I tell Katie about my first game here and about the young uncles whom she knows and loves as old men. I wonder if the cancer will kill me before they are gone. I wonder if maybe, even now, I am sitting in the same seat I sat in 50 years before.

I think of the pictures Katie and I just took of each other, and I remember a black and white photograph from Cedar Crest days, a little boy with a 15-inch bat on the shoulder of a striped polo shirt, one strap broken on his short pants overalls, a slight frown of concentration on his face, a lot of blond hair on his head. I wonder if there is anything left of that little boy in this bald, cancerous, middle-aged man. I decide that there is still one thing that holds us together and makes us one. We are both loved by God and Grandma and baseball and the uncles. I think I must be in the same green seat.

note

[1]Marty Brenneman and Joe Nuxhall are Reds radio and television reporters. Waite Hoyt, a Hall of Fame pitcher for the Yankees, was the Reds radio announcer when I was growing up.

leaving Chrisney,
going downhill

The young woman at the hardware store pointed to the cin-
derblock building, down a few empty shop fronts and across
the street.

"Bob and Catherine run the 'service center' over there.
It's a little bit of a store and more of a restaurant. The old
men go there to drink coffee and argue."

"I'll fit right in," I said.

I look like an old man, even though I'm not, and I can
argue a little. I hadn't returned for drinking or arguing,
though. I wasn't sure why I'd come, except it was on the way
I was traveling, the way home, the first time I'd been down
that road for 36 years.

As I crossed the street, I pulled out the mental picture of
Bob and Catherine Adams as they were when I left Chrisney
36 years before—the young parents of three children. She
was little and cute and dark-haired. He was muscular and
flat-topped and energetic.

She's still little and cute, although stooped now, too. He's
still flat-topped. That's all the years since the fall of '56
haven't changed.

I didn't expect them to recognize me. The years have
changed me, too. I wasn't bald and white-bearded and carrying 30 pounds of marriage then. So I told them who I was,
the 19-year-old college sophomore who had been sent to fill
in on weekends until the regularly appointed pastor graduated from seminary. (I was full of call and confidence in
those days. After all, I had taken Speech 101 and possessed a
stack of my grandmother's old *Reader's Digests*.

I didn't really expect them to remember me. I had been
there for only three months, just weekends, a lifetime ago. I
didn't know a thing about a big church like Chrisney, its

hundred members twice as many as my home church could boast. My preaching certainly was forgettable; I hadn't yet discovered how to steal from Harry Emerson Fosdick.

Bob and Catherine Adams had been uncommonly kind to me before I had left Chrisney, inviting me into their home and family for Friday and Saturday night suppers. I wanted to thank them for their kindness, make up for 36 years of absence. I also wanted to let them see that I'd done alright since leaving Chrisney, let them know that their teaching had borne fruit. I knew that in their minds there had to be some question about that.

To my amazement, they remembered me immediately.

"Of course," said Catherine. "You're the 'knothead.'"

We talked about families and showed pictures. (Catherine said she didn't really need to see a picture of my wife; she knew she'd be pretty. I showed her one anyway. She was pleased at her prescience.)

We reminisced about the people in the church in the fall of '56. I learned the fates of the other two churches on the circuit—Crossroads and Bloomfield. (I couldn't remember which country road to take to find Crossroads, and they wouldn't tell me. "It's been closed a long time. Hay stored in it. Wouldn't want you to see it that way.")

They explained about the "service center," their stock of brooms and odds and ends, the eclectic and eccentric chairs and tables, the counter for serving sandwiches and Methodist Moonshine (a corrosive and hundred-proof brew known in its lesser forms as "coffee").

"We're too old to stay here and run this place," Catherine said, "but these old retired guys don't have any place to go. They get on their wives' nerves so when they're home all the time. I guess it's just our contribution to keeping the divorce rate down."

Bob laughed. "You should see the gifts she gets at Christmas from those women!"

We spoke of meals shared and lessons learned so long ago. I recalled the parsonage in which I had lived from Friday evening to Sunday afternoon.

Thinking of that house made me hear again the uncertain steps of Bob Adams on the parsonage porch that dark Friday night. As they echoed in my memory, I knew why I had left Chrisney as I did, why Bob and Catherine had a right to question my call, and why I had now returned.

For 36 years I had carried the guilt, yes, even the shame, of that night, like a well-hidden millstone around the neck of my ministry, carried it ever since I left Chrisney 2,000 sermons ago.

Now I had to say it, my eyes searching the oil-cloth of the little lunchtime table: "Do you remember when Billy Quick was killed?"

"Yes, of course," said Catherine. "How could we forget that?"

I knew just how she felt.

Their faces, however, had changed. Big smiles suddenly brought back images of those young parents and earnest church members of 36 years before.

"You know, Billy's father was one of our good friends. Up until the day he died, he talked about how you came to their house that night, and how much you comforted them. He said you knew just the right words to say—something about a rose."

As I drove away, going down the big hill north of town, I realized they hadn't even asked about my ministry over the 36 years since I left Chrisney. I really had intended to brag to them about the large and impressive churches served (the large ones were not always the impressive ones), the learned societies and solemn assemblies addressed, the articles published, the honors garnered, the doctorate earned. I wanted to assure them, or perhaps to assure myself, that I really had been called, that the start of my ministry had not been its only measure, that I had been "successful," despite that October evening in '56. But they hadn't even asked.

Then I understood. They didn't need to know any more. I hadn't *become* a success. For them, I had always been as good as I would ever be. They didn't see me through the haze of education and acclaim; they saw me through the eyes of grace.

They aren't silly people, the kind who think the surest sign of the presence of God is some emotional slush, with a rhyme to hold it down. They know that an experienced pastor with good skills is better than a kid with some sentimental tripe. They also know God uses what's at hand.

They didn't need to know about degrees and awards, because they already knew God could use me, even me. Good church members always understand something that clergy occasionally forget: the only thing that really makes a pastor is the grace of God.

So Bob and Catherine didn't need to ask about my "career." They had been present for the greatest success I would ever have, because it wasn't my success at all. I've been going downhill ever since leaving Chrisney. I reached the pinnacle right there in front of them, as the 19-year-old knothead who, by the grace of God, said just the right thing to the family of Billy Quick.

in the balcony,
not being @ bishop

I was sitting in the balcony when it occurred to me that I
will never be a bishop. It was a Sunday afternoon, a gathering of congregations from around the area. We were in a
church larger than mine, pastored by a man younger than I.
We were listening to a sermon by our bishop, a man a few
months younger than I, a man of great charm and spirit, a
man who possessed a vastly inferior education.[1] That's when
I thought of it, really, for the first time. I'm always going to
be in the balcony. I'm never going to be a bishop.

It shouldn't have been such a surprise. After all, my
"career" came to a sliding halt years ago. Oh, I've been pastoring all the time since then, been at work, but my "career"?
That ended a long time ago. I didn't know it then, of course.

In my early years of ministry, however, I was often told
that I would someday be a bishop, by Aunt Nora . . . Mr.
Heathman . . . Dallas Browning . . . I was, after all, that most
dangerous of persons, "a promising young man." It's an anxious occupation, being promising, because everyone expects
you to keep the promises, but no one tells you what they are.
I knew, though. My promise, my destiny, was to be a bishop.

Surely anyone else could have told you years before that
day I sat in the balcony that I would never be a bishop. My
days of promise were long over. Bishops aren't elected from
the ranks of small town pastors. Nobody bothered to mention to *me*, however, that I would never be a bishop, so I just
kept on assuming . . . assuming that I would someday be
Richard Raines.

That's who my bishop was, for as long as I could remember. There were no term limitations on bishops in those
days. Richard Campbell Raines was bishop of the Methodist
Church in Indiana for 20 years. He was the first bishop I

ever heard of, when I was 14. He ordained me when I was 27. He was my bishop.

He probably wasn't more than 5'9", but he was always taller than anyone he was with, including me, and I'm 6'1". He was ramrod straight. I still remember him at his retirement celebration, on a stage in front of several hundred people, playing the piano for his own party because the organizers hadn't remembered to get an accompanist for the songs. In the evening ballroom light from where we sat, his handsome shock of white hair looked blond. He sat so uprightly on the bench, you would have sworn he was a boy in his teens.

He was charming and gracious, a scholar, a pastor, and most of all a preacher. In the pulpit his arms were so long, it was like he could reach out to where you sat and tip your head over and simply pour the words into your ear.

It is hard to be loved as a bishop in the Methodist tradition. Our bishops have absolute power over pastoral appointments. Any pastor goes wherever the bishop sends him or her. Any congregation accepts whoever the bishop sends. A bishop might be respected, but rarely loved. Richard Raines was respected. He was also loved.

The autumn after his retirement I invited him to lead a weekend retreat for the students of my campus ministry.

"I don't know," he said. "You'd better get someone younger. I live in the present age, but the present age doesn't live in me."

This was a man who just that summer, at age 70, finally had time to learn to water-ski, so he did. We insisted he come, present age or not. He did. It was the best thing I ever did for those students.

It is said that when old men become irrelevant, young men become irresponsible. Richard Raines was always relevant to me. He kept me responsible. It was no easy task.

Why I kept getting into trouble in my early years of ministry, I'm not exactly sure. Of course, I kept getting into trouble all along the way, so perhaps it was just consistency. But in those days I had no tenure. I was still "on trial." If a District Superintendent got mad at me, and there were several who had good reason, he could drop me out of the system. Whenever that happened, I would go to Bishop Raines. The bishop always interceded for me.

I remember a full professor of English at the University of California at Berkeley in the 1960s telling about how he had participated in a campus demonstration. "I yelled at the president," he said. "It was the first time in all my years there I'd ever had a chance to speak to him." I think perhaps I got into so much trouble just so I could see my bishop once in a while.

One thing I learned, then and many other times through the years, often from District Superintendents, is that administrators are not in place to solve your problems. They are there to solve their problems. You get them to solve your problem in either of two ways: (1) You line up your problem with their problem, so they can't help but solve yours as they solve theirs; or (2) you become a problem to them.

I was a problem to Richard Raines, but he always acted like it was one he was glad to have.

I just always assumed I would one day grow up and be a relevant old man instead of an irresponsible young one. I always assumed I would be a bishop.

Did I think, somewhere down deep, that being a bishop would confirm my strange call to ministry? Probably so. After all, I spent my career wondering if I had really been called. There were plenty of folk along the way who were willing to stoke that doubt. If I became a bishop, though, wouldn't that be the final seal, the affirmation that I had indeed been called, that I hadn't just masqueraded as a minister all those years?

I had sat alone in the balcony that day, surrounded by friends, but still alone. My wife was at home grading papers. She was the only one who might know what I still expected.

"I'm never going to be a bishop," I said to her over supper. "I realized that today at the district meeting. I'm a little embarrassed. I don't know why I ever thought . . . especially in these last few years why I kept thinking . . . I mean, everybody but me must have known for a long time. . . ."

Helen is a gracious and grace-full woman, in the proper sense of grace as a gift of love one does not merit and has not earned. Her presence is always grace for me, and her words almost always are. It was surely grace that allowed her to see what my real goal was when I didn't know it myself, and it was only grace, not the facts, that allowed her to come to such a conclusion.

"You just got it a little off-target," she said. "You never really wanted to be a bishop. You wanted to be Richard Raines. The young pastors now, when they get into trouble, who do they come to? They come to you. You chose the better part. You're not a bishop, but you *are* Richard Raines."

notes

[1]There is a small amount of competition among seminaries . . . well, okay, there's quite a bit at times. Bishop Woodie W. White went to Boston; I went to Garrett. When I was at Garrett, one of our professors, Samuel Lauechli, liked to tell about the student who transferred from Garrett to Boston and in so doing raised the level of both institutions.

glossary

All church terms refer to the United Methodist Church (1968–present) or to the Methodist Church (1939–1968).

Annual Conference—Both an organizational/regional unit and the annual meeting of that organizational/regional unit. It covers all the congregations in a certain geographical area, is divided into districts, and is presided over by a bishop. The ministers of the Annual Conference and lay members from each church within the Conference meet annually to transact business, ordain new ministers, and worship together.

Area or Episcopal Area—The province of a bishop, usually including one or two annual conferences. *Episcopos* is the Greek word for bishop, hence "episcopal."

Bishop—An ordained elder who is elected at a meeting of a jurisdictional conference and assigned to an episcopal area for a quadrennium. She or he is elected for life but can serve one area for only two quadrennia.

Charge—The church or churches in the care of one pastor. (I started on "three-point" charges, meaning I had three churches.)

Charge Conference—The annual business meeting of a congregation, presided over by the District Superintendent.

Circuit—A multichurch charge.

Clergy—Pastors, priests, ministers, ordained persons.

Deacon—*See* Elder.

District—An organizational and geographical subdivision of an annual conference made up of 30 to 90 congregations, according to how many churches are available in a certain geographical region, and presided over by a district superintendent. Where there are many United Methodist churches, a district might cover a fairly small geographical area, such as five or six counties. There are 20 districts in the two annual conferences in the state of Illinois, whereas the state of Wyoming is a district of the Rocky Mountain Conference. **District Superintendent (D.S.)**—A denominational official who is an ordained clergyperson appointed by the Bishop for a term of six years. She or he is the direct supervisor of pastors and congregations for a district, serving under the direction of the Bishop. In recent times there has been a move toward calling persons in this office "conference superintendents," although they are still assigned to a district. (In the church, changes in names are often confused with renewal.)

Elder—Until 1996 the second of two ordinations. The first was as a deacon. The ordination as deacon emphasized service (servanthood) and was a step on the way to full ordination as an elder. The ordination as elder emphasizes the spiritual leadership of "word and sacrament." In 1996 the General Conference dropped ordination as deacon as a step to ordination as elder.

Episcopal—The word means "pertaining to a bishop." So, the old Methodist Episcopal Church meant "the Methodist church with bishops," as contrasted with the Methodist Protestant Church, which did not have bishops. An "episcopal area" means the area presided over by a bishop. In Methodist terms, "episcopal" has nothing to do with the Protestant Episcopal Church, or Episcopalians.

Episcopal Area—The area presided over by a bishop; usually made up of one or two annual conferences.

General Conference—An equal number of lay and clergy representatives elected by their annual conferences who meet once each quadrennium to transact the business of the United Methodist Church and make any necessary (or unnecessary) changes in the theology, order, discipline, and bureaucracy of the church.

Historic Protestant Denominations—Often called "mainline denominations," although I prefer to call them "full circle churches." They include American Baptist, Christian

(Disciples of Christ), Episcopal, Lutheran (not Missouri Synod or Wisconsin Synod), Methodist, Presbyterian, and United Church of Christ (a merger of the Congregational and Evangelical and Reformed denominations). Others often included are the Reformed Church in America, the Christian Reformed Church, Mennonites, Moravians, and several African-American denominations.

Indiana University (IU)—The main state university in Indiana, it contains many branches. The branch locations are designated by another letter after the initials, such as IUSB for Indiana University at South Bend. I always refer to the first, and main, campus at Bloomington, which is sometimes called IUB.

Intervarsity Christian Fellowship (IV)—A nondenominational campus religious organization.

Jurisdictional Conference—A region of annual conferences, usually made up of several states. Delegates from each annual conference in the jurisdiction meet each quadrennium, primarily to elect bishops.

Laity/Laypersons—Non-ordained members of the church.

Lay Pastor—Someone without formal education but who is considered to have adequate gifts and graces to "fill the pulpit" when there is an inadequate supply of educated pastors. Usually they are not ordained, meaning they cannot serve communion or baptize, although there are provisions for what is called "local" ordination.

License to Preach—Certification for a layperson to act as pastor of a charge; also called "license as a local pastor."

Mainline Denominations—*See* Historic Protestant Denominations.

Methodist Church, The—Formed in 1939 by the merger of the Methodist Episcopal Church, the Methodist Episcopal Church South, and the Methodist Protestant Church. Episcopal means "led by bishops." The two Methodist Episcopal Churches had split over slavery. The Methodist Protestant Church had split off because it did not believe in bishops. In

1968 the Methodist Church merged with the Evangelical United Brethren Church to form the United Methodist Church.

Parsonage—The house provided by the congregation for a pastor to live. In some denominations, Presbyterian especially, it's called a "manse." The home of a Roman Catholic or Episcopal priest is usually called the "rectory."

PK—Preacher's Kid. (My children usually referred to themselves as **TOs**, for Theologian's Offspring.)

Quadrennium—A four-year period.

Seminary—A professional theological school for educating ministers. In the historic Protestant denominations it is a three-year graduate program following a four-year undergraduate degree.

United Methodist Church (UMC)—Formed in 1968 by the union of the Methodist Church and the Evangelical United Brethren Church.

U OF I—University of Illinois.

Wesley Foundation (WF)—The Methodist (pre-1968) or United Methodist (after 1968) campus ministry unit at a tax-supported institution of higher education. At private colleges and universities it is usually called the Methodist Student Movement.

Wesley, John—(1703–1791) A priest of the Church of England who founded the Methodist movement, which he saw as an attempt to revitalize the Church of England rather than as the formation of a separate denomination. His brother, **Charles,** was a hymn writer who was responsible for many of the hymns still sung in many churches.

Woman's Society of Christian Service (WSCS)—The women's organization from 1939 to1968.